SAY IT IN
HINDI

by
Veena Talwar Oldenburg

Dover Publications, Inc.
New York

This volume in the Dover *Say It* series was prepared under the editorial supervision of Nancy D. Gross.

Special thanks to Mr. Martin Tytell, of Tytell Typewriters, N.Y.C., for his painstaking preparation of the Hindi typewriter used in this book.

Published in Canada by General Publishing Company, Ltd., 30 Lesmill Road, Don Mills, Toronto, Ontario.
Published in the United Kingdom by Constable and Company, Ltd.

Say It in Hindi is a new work, first published by Dover Publications, Inc., in 1981.

International Standard Book Number: 0-486-23959-4
Library of Congress Catalog Card Number: 80-65376

Manufactured in the United States of America
Dover Publications, Inc.
31 East 2nd Street
Mineola, New York 11501

CONTENTS

INTRODUCTION

Say It in Hindi is based on the form of Hindi spoken in the north central part of India, which encompasses the capital city of New Delhi, Agra (the city of the Taj Mahal) and Lucknow, a city with many literary and historical associations. Hindi is the most prevalent of India's fourteen official languages, being the native tongue of almost 40% of the population. Hindi is the native language of much of north and central India, but it is taught on a nationwide basis and understood almost everywhere. It is the official language of all government business, broadcasting and notices in the part of India visited by tourists and business people most often.

Hindi is written in a syllabic script called *Devanagari* from left to right, as is English. The script is based on an ancient classical language, Sanskrit, as are the technical and literary words in pure Hindi.

There is a very closely related North Indian language called Urdu, which is spoken by Indian Muslims, educated, upper class North Indians and is the official language of Pakistan. Urdu is written from right to left in a script derived from the Arabic and Persian alphabets, and these two languages are the source of its learned vocabulary.

The grammar, everyday vocabulary and language of Hindi and Urdu are for all practical purposes identical. Therefore, this book is designed to facilitate oral communication with a large majority of the inhabitants of the Indian subcontinent. With almost 300 million native speakers of Hindi/Urdu (sometimes referred as Hindustani) and many millions more who use Hindi as a secondary language, *Say It in Hindi* will enable you to

reach more people than any other language in the world
with the exception of Chinese.

NOTES ON THE USE OF THIS BOOK

This book is divided into sections which cover the
various situations and topics encountered by the traveller.
While the entries in most sections of this book follow
English alphabetical order, the list of Indian food specialties is alphabetized according to the Hindi words to
allow for easy reference and quick recognition in restaurants.

An index is provided at the end of the book which
forms an instant English-Hindi glossary. It can refer the
user to the necessary consecutively numbered entry
immediately.

It is not the purpose of the present book to explain
the points of Hindi grammar. But it is impossible to
write a Hindi phrasebook which is of wide practical
application without taking several major features of the
Hindi language into account.

Nouns in Hindi are either masculine or feminine. The
verb and adjective endings agree in gender with the
grammatical subject of the sentence. We have indicated,
wherever necessary, both the masculine and feminine
verb forms thusly:

> I want to see [your superior].
> maĩ [aap ké afsar] sé milnaa [chaahataa (M.)]
>   [chaahatee (F.)] hoon.

In the above sentence, the (M.) indicates that the verb
form which precedes it in brackets should be used along
with a masculine subject, while the one followed by (F.)
should be used for a feminine subject. In this case, the

subject is identical with the speaker and the form would be determined by the sex of the speaker.

Adjectives also alternate in the same manner. This book has been designed so that if the format of the phrases and substitutions is followed, the agreement of adjectives with the nouns will automatically be correct. Inanimate nouns, which can be either masculine or feminine, have also been provided with proper verb and adjective forms in the context of the sentences. For variant forms of nouns, verbs and adjectives, consult the index.

The material in this book has been selected chiefly to teach you many essential phrases, sentences and questions for travel. It will serve as a direct and interesting introduction to the spoken language if you are beginning your study. The sentences will be useful to you whether or not you go on to further study. With the aid of a dictionary, many sentence patterns included here will answer innumerable needs, for example: "She has lost [her handbag]." The brackets indicate that substitutions can be made for these words with the use of a bilingual dictionary. In other sentences, for the words in square brackets you can substitute the words immediately following (in the same sentence or in the indented entries below it). For example, the entry

> Turn [left] [right] at the next corner.

provides two sentences: "Turn left at the next corner" and "Turn right at the next corner." Three sentences are provided by the entry

> Give me a seat [on the aisle].
> —by a window.
> —by the emergency exit.

As your Hindi vocabulary grows, you will find that you

can express an increasingly wide range of thoughts by the proper substitution of words in these model sentences.

Please note that whereas brackets always indicate the possibility of substitutions, parentheses have been used to indicate synonyms or alternative usage for an entry, such as:

How are you (OR: How do you do)?

The alternate usage is preceded by (OR:).

Parentheses within brackets have been used to indicate different forms of the same verb which vary according to gender (as described above). Different forms of nouns for male and female are indicated in the same way:

Give my regards to [your friend].
[apné dost (M.)] [apnee sahélee (F.)] sé meraa namasté kéhnaa.

Variations in words according to number as well are indicated where necessary thus:

The first.
[péhlaa (M.)] [péhlee (F.)] [péhlé (PL.)]

with (PL.) for *plural* indicating the word is referring to more than one thing or person.

Occasionally, parentheses are used to clarify a word or to explain some nuance of meaning that may be implicit or understood in either the English or the Hindi phrase. The abbreviation "(LIT.)" is used whenever a literal translation of a Hindi phrase or sentence is supplied.

You will notice that the word "please" has been omitted from many of the English sentences. This was done merely to make them shorter and clearer, and to avoid repetition. Most of the Hindi sentences in this book use the polite forms of verbs so you do not have to worry about adding the word "please" to any phrase. If you wish to be extra polite, you may use the equivalents for "please" listed in the index, at the beginning of any sentence.

You will find the extensive index at the end of the book especially helpful. Capitalized items in the index refer to section and subsection headings and give the number of the page on which the section begins. All other numbers refer to *entry numbers*. All the entries in the book are numbered consecutively. With the aid of the index, you will find many words and phrases at a glance.

PRONUNCIATION

We have supplied an explanatory chart of the transcription system used in this book to aid you in correct pronunciation. Read over the notes carefully so you may become familiar with the sounds of Hindi and the phonetic transcription.

Many Hindi consonants and vowels have counterparts in English. Those that do not are explained in the notes. Hindi makes several distinctions in the pronunciation of consonants that are not taken into account in English. Hindi distinguishes between those consonants which end with a strong puff of breath (aspirated consonants) and those that end with no puff of breath at all (unaspirated consonants). For example, *t* is contrasted with *th* in the words *tak* "until" and *thak* "tired," on the basis of aspiration alone. It is important to maintain this difference, as it is often the only one in two otherwise identical words.

Another important feature of Hindi is the sharp division of consonants according to the position of the tongue in relation to the other parts of the mouth when a particular sound is produced. This should be observed carefully, especially in the case of the sounds *T, TH, D, DH* and *t, th, d, dh*. The first set of sounds is produced with the tongue in the same position as for the English equivalents, against the middle of the roof of the mouth, but the tip of the tongue is pointed backwards towards the throat. This is called retroflexion, and the first set of consonants is called retroflex consonants. The second set of consonants is pronounced as the English equivalents, but the tip of the tongue is pushed forward against the back of the upper teeth, and thus referred to as dental consonants. The only indication of a difference in meaning between the words *kaTnaa* "to be cut" and *katnaa* "to be spun," for example, is the proper placement of the tongue. The distinction between retroflex and dental consonants should be rigorously observed in Hindi, or it could lead to some rather embarrassing misunderstandings. Practice producing these sounds and also try recognizing them in speech.

Stress is much less important in Hindi than in English. Generally, stress follows vowel length. Those syllables which contain long vowels are emphasized slightly, but this is practically automatic if you make sure to give the proper length and quality to the vowels of each syllable. In order to facilitate this, the Hindi words have been broken into syllables, which are separated by hyphens.

Pay close attention to the transcription at first. Do not be misled by the words borrowed from English which appear in this book. Hindi has taken the words, but it has imparted its own unique pronunciation to them. If you pronounce these English loanwords just as you would when conversing with another English speaker, very few Hindi speakers will be able to understand you. Follow the transcription for all the phrases, regardless of how familiar a word may *seem*.

Because this transcription can serve at best only as an approximation of correct pronunciation, ultimate precision and consistency have very occasionally been sacrificed for simplicity and ease of comprehension. The more conscientiously you follow the transcription, the better your chances of getting your ideas across. You will discover that there are probably no sounds in Hindi that you cannot pronounce with a little practice and, using this book as a tool, you will be surprised at how well you will be able to make yourself understood.

CONSONANTS

Hindi letter	Tran- scription	Remarks
क्	k	pronounced as *k* in s*k*it with no puff of air.
क़	*q	pronounced as *k* but farther back in the mouth, with the back of the tongue making a clicking or popping sound against the opening of the throat passage.
ख्	kh	pronounced as *k* in *k*it with very strong puff of air.
ख़	*kh	pronounced as *ch* in Scottish lo*ch* or German a*ch*.
ग्	g	pronounced as *g* in le*g*al with no puff of air.
ग़	*gh	pronounced as French *r* in su*r*, or like a dry gargling sound from the back of the throat.
घ्	gh	pronounced as *g* in *g*et with very strong puff of air.
ञ्	n	pronounced as *n* in *n*ow.
च्	ch	pronounced as *ch* in tea*ch*er with no puff of air.

* These letters —q, *kh*, *gh*, z, f— occur in words of Arabic or Persian origin. Many speakers maintain these sounds in their speech, but others often pronounce them as k, kh, g, j and ph, respectively.

ਛ	chh	pronounced as *ch* in *ch*urch with very strong puff of air.
ज	j	pronounced as *j* in ad*j*ust with no puff of air.
ज़	*z	pronounced as z in zoo.
झ	jh	pronounced as *j* in *j*ack with very strong puff of air.
ञ	n	pronounced as *n* in *n*ow.
ट	T	pronounced as *t* in *t*ouch but with tip of tongue touching roof of mouth and pointed backward towards throat, with no puff of air.
ठ	TH	pronounced the same way as *T,* but with very strong puff of air; never as *th* in *th*e or *th*eater.
ड	D	pronounced as *d* in *d*og but with tip of tongue touching roof of mouth and pointed backward towards throat, with no puff of air.
ढ	DH	pronounced the same as *D,* but with very strong puff of air.
ण	N	pronounced as *n* in bar*n* with tip of tongue pointing backward.
त	t	pronounced as *t* in s*t*ake but with tip of tongue pressed against back of upper teeth, with no puff of air.
थ	th	pronounced as *t* in *t*ake but with tip of tongue pressed against back of upper teeth, with very strong puff of air; never as *th* in *th*e or *th*eater.

द	d	pronounced as *d* in a*d*mit but with tip of tongue pressed against back of upper teeth, with no puff of air.
घ	dh	pronounced as *d* in *d*og but with tip of tongue pressed against back of upper teeth, with very strong puff of air.
न	n	pronounced as *n* in *n*ow.
प	p	pronounced as *p* in s*p*ike with no puff of air.
फ	ph	pronounced as *p* in *p*ike with very strong puff of air; never as *ph* in *ph*otograph.
फ़	*f	pronounced as *f* in *f*oot.
ब	b	pronounced as *b* in ta*b*le with no puff of air.
भ	bh	pronounced as *b* in *b*at with very strong puff of air.
म	m	pronounced as *m* in *m*ine.
य	y	pronounced as *y* in *y*es.
र	r	pronounced as *r* in British ve*r*y or as in o*r*der.
ड़	R	pronounced as *D* but the tip of the tongue does not quite touch the roof of the mouth; instead it is very quickly flapped from its backward-pointing position to the back of the lower teeth.
ढ़	RH	pronounced as *R* but with very strong puff of air.
ल	l	pronounced as *l* in *l*ove.

व	v	pronounced as *v* in *v*oice.
ष	sh	pronounced as *sh* in *sh*ip.
श	sh	pronounced as *sh* in *sh*ip.
स	s	pronounced as *s* in *s*it.
ह	h	at the end of a syllable or word, pronounced as just a strong puff of air; elsewhere as *h* in *h*at.

VOWELS

Vowels are considered long or short in Hindi but they are grouped differently than in English. The vowels below are arranged according to Hindi conventions to aid the user in proper placement of stress.

SHORT VOWELS

Hindi letter	Transcription	Remarks
अ	a	pronounced as *a* in *a*bout or as *u* in b*u*t.
	é	following an *h* sound, often pronounced as *é* in French *é*té or as *a* in f*a*ce with abrupt ending.
इ	i	pronounced as *i* in b*i*t.
उ	u	pronounced as *u* in p*u*t.

LONG VOWELS

| आ | aa | pronounced as *a* in f*a*ther. |
| ई | ee | pronounced as *ee* in s*ee*. |

ऊ	oo	pronounced as *oo* in b*oo*t.
ए	é	pronounced as above.
ऐ	ai	pronounced as halfway between the *e* in p*e*t and the *a* in p*a*t; for some speakers as *ai* in *ai*sle.
ओ	o	pronounced as *o* in n*o*te.
औ	au	pronounced as *au* in s*au*ce.

NASALIZED VOWELS

Special attention should be paid to the nasalized vowels in Hindi, since they indicate differences in meaning and grammatical function and have no counterparts in English. Phonetically, they are made very much like the French nasal vowels: the breath passes through both the nose and mouth when a nasalized vowel is formed, instead of just through the mouth as in ordinary vowels. Do not move your tongue or change the position of your jaw when you say these vowels.

If you find it hard to catch the nasal sounds and to imitate them, try to sound English vowels while "talking through your nose" as children do. You may find that breaking off the vowel suddenly will make the nasalization easier for you to imitate.

In general, when you make these nasalized vowels, *you do not pronounce the accompanying n*; it is simply an indication of nasalization. The letter *n* has been introduced into the transcription to alert the beginner to the formation of previously unfamiliar nasalized sounds.

Theoretically, any Hindi vowel can be nasalized but in practice only the long vowels are true nasals. They are as follows:

Hindi letter	Transcription
आं	aan
ईं	een
ऊं	oon
एं	én
ऐं	ain
ओं	on
औं	aun

HINDI SPELLING

When the vowel sounds occur in isolation, as the initial sound of a word or immediately following another vowel, they are written with the characters described above.

More frequently the vowels are written in combination with the preceding consonants. Take for example, *k*:

Hindi letters	Transcription
क	ka (short *a* is considered inherent in the consonant sign)
का	kaa
कि	ki
की	kee
कु	ku
कू	koo
के	ké

कै   kai

को   ko

कौ   kau

Nasalized vowels are indicated by ꙶ or • over the consonant sign:

कां   k$\overline{\text{aan}}$

कीं   k$\overline{\text{een}}$

and so forth.

EVERYDAY PHRASES

1. Hello (OR: **Goodbye***).
na-mas-té.   नमस्ते ।

2. Welcome
aa-i-yé.   आइये ।

3. See you later.
phir mi-len-gé.   फिर मिलेंगे ।

4. Yes.
jee haan.   जी हाँ ।

5. No.
jee na-heen.   जी नहीं ।

6. Perhaps (OR: **Maybe**).
shaa-yad.   शायद ।

7. Please.
kri-paa ho-gee (OR: mé-hér-baa-nee kar-ké).
कृपया होगी (मेहरबानी करके) ।

8. Allow me.
i-jaa-zat dén.   इजाज़त दें ।

9. Excuse me (OR: **Pardon me**).
ksha-maa kee-ji-yé (OR: maaf kee-ji-yé).
क्षमा कीजिये (माफ़ कीजिये) ।

10. Thanks [very much].
[ba-hut] dhan-ya-vaad.   [बहुत] घन्यवाद ।

> * Greetings do not vary at different times of the day; accompanied by the gesture of joined palms this word is the accepted form of greeting or parting at all times of the day.

11. You are welcome (OR: **Don't mention it**).
ko-ee baat na-heen.   कोई बात नहीं ।

12. All right (OR: **Very good**).
ach-chhaa (OR: ba-hut ach-chhaa).
अच्छा (बहुत अच्छा) ।

13. It doesn't matter.
ko-ee baat na-heen.   कोई बात नहीं ।

14. Don't bother.
aap kashT na ka-ren.   आप कष्ट न करें ।

15. I am sorry.
mu-jhé af-sos hai.   मुझे अफ़्सोस है ।

16. You have been [very kind].
aap kee [ba-hut kri-paa].   आप की [बहुत कृपा] ।

17. You have [helped] me a lot.
aap né ba-hut [ma-dad kee].   आप ने बहुत [मदद की] ।

18. Come in.
an-dar aa-i-yé.   अन्दर आइये ।

19. Come here.
i-dhar aa-i-yé.   इधर आइये ।

20. Come with me.
mé-ré saath aa-i-yé.   मेरे साथ आइये ।

21. Come back later.
kuchh dér men vaa-pas aa-i-yé.
कुछ देर मैं वापस आइये ।

22. Come early.
jal-dee aa-i-yé.   जल्दी आइये ।

23. Wait a bit.
za-raa THa-he-ri-yé. ज़रा ठहरिये ।

24. Wait for us.
ha-maa-raa in-té-zaar kee-ji-yé.
हमारा इन्तेज़ार कीजिये ।

25. Not yet.
a-bhee tak na-heen. अभी तक नहीं ।

26. Not now.
a-bhee na-heen. अभी नहीं ।

27. Listen.
su-ni-yé. सुनिये ।

28. Look out.
dé-khi-yé. देखिये ।

29. Be careful.
saav-dhaan (OR: dhyaan sé).
सावधान (ध्यान से) ।

SOCIAL PHRASES

30. Meet [Mrs. Singh].
[shree-ma-tee sing] sé mi-li-yé.*
[श्रीमती सिंह] से मिलिये ।

31. —Miss Manju.*
—ku-maa-ree man-joo. _ कुमारी मन्जू ।

* Unmarried women are most commonly addressed by their
first names.

32. —Mr. Saran.

—shree sa-ran. _ श्री सरन।

33. Pleased to meet you.

aap sé mil kar *khu*-shee hu-ee.

आप से मिल कर ख़ुशी हुई।

34. How are you (OR: How do you do)?

(aap) kai-sé hain (OR: kyaa haal hai)?

(आप) कैसे है॰ (क्या हाल है)?

35. Very well, thanks, and you?

THeek hoon, aur aap? ठीक हूँ, और आप?

36. All right (OR: Fine).

[ach-chhaa (M.)] [ach-chhee (F.)] (OR: THeek) hoon.

[अच्छा] [अच्छी] (ठीक) हूँ।

37. So, So.

ai-sé hee hai. ऐसे ही है।

38. What's new?

ko-ee taa-zee *kha*-bar? कोई ताज़ी ख़बर?

39. Please sit down (OR: Take a seat).

bai-THi-yé (OR: tash-reef ra-khi-yé).

बैठिये (तशरीफ़ रखिये)।

40. It's a pleasure to see you again.

aap sé phir mil kar ba-hut *khu*-shee hu-ee.

आप से फिर मिल कर बहुत ख़ुशी हुई।

41. Congratulations.

mu-baa-rak ho (OR: ba-dhaa-ee). मुबारक हो (बधाई)।

42. I like you very much.

aap mu-jhé ba-hut pa-sand hain.

आप मुझे बहुत पसन्द है॰।

43. I love you.
main aap sé prém [kar-taa (M.)] [kar-tee (F.)] hoon.
मैं आप से प्रेम [करता] [करती] हूं।

44. May I see you again?
aap sé phir mu-laa-qaat ho-gee na?
आप से फिर मुलाक़ात होगी ना?

45. Let's make a date for next week.
ag-lé haf-té mil-né kaa sa-may tay kar lén.
आले हफ़्ते मिलने का समय तय कर लें।

46. I have enjoyed myself very much.
mu-jhé ba-hut ma-zaa aa-yaa.   मुझे बहुत मज़ा आया।

47. Give my regards to [your friend].
[ap-né dost (M.)] [ap-nee sa-hé-lee (F.)] sé mé-raa na-mas-té kéh-naa.
[अपने दोस्त] [अपनी सहेली] से मेरा नमस्ते कहना।

BASIC QUESTIONS

48. What?
kyaa? क्या?

49. What did you say?
aap né kyaa ka-haa? आप ने क्या कहा?

50. What is [this] [that]?
[yé] [vo] kyaa hai? [यह][वह] क्या है?

51. What shall I do?
main kyaa ka-roon? मैं क्या करूं?

52. What is the matter?
kyaa baat hai? क्या बात है?

53. What do you want?
aap ko kyaa chaa-hi-yé? आप को क्या चाहिये?

54. When?
kab? कब?

55. When does it [leave]?
vo kab [jaa-yé-gaa (M.)] [jaa-yé-gee (F.)]?*
वह कब [जायेगा] [जायेगी]?

56. —arrive.
—[aa-yé-gaa (M.)] [aa-yé-gee (F.)].*
_   [आयेगा] [आयेगी]।

57. —begin.
—[shu-roo ho-gaa (M.)] [shu-roo ho-gee (F.)].*
_   [शुरू होगा] [शुरू होगी]।

58. —end.
—[sa-maapt ho-gaa (M.)] [sa-maapt ho-gee (F.)].*
_   [समाप्त होगा] [समाप्त होगी]।

59. Where?
ka-haan? कहाँ?

60. Where to?
ki-dhar? किधर?

61. Why?
kyon? क्यों?

62. How?
kai-sé? कैसे?

---

* Depends on whether the noun to which "it" refers to is masculine or feminine in gender.

63. How long?
kit-nee dér (OR: kab tak)? कितनी देर (कब तक)?

64. How far?
kit-nee door? कितनी दूर?

65. How much?
kit-naa? कितना?

66. How many?
kit-né? कितने?

67. How do you do it?
aap kai-sé [kar-té (M.)] [kar-tee (F.)] hain?
आप क्या [करते] [करती] हैं?

68. How does it work?
yé kai-sé kaam [kar-taa (M.)] [kar-tee (F.)] hai?
यह कैसे काम [करता] [करती] है?

69. Who?
kaun? कौन?

70. Who are you?
aap kaun hain? आप कौन हैं?

71. Who is [that boy]?
[vo laR-kaa] kaun hai? [वह लड़का] कौन है?

72. —that girl.
—vo laR-kee. _ वह लड़की ।

73. —this man.
—yé aad-mee. _ यह आदमी ।

74. —this woman.
—yé au-rat. _ यह औरत ।

75. Am I [on time] [early] [late]?
kyaa main [THeek sa-may par] [jal-dee] [dér sé] hoon?
क्या मै॰ [ठीक समय पर] [जल्दी] [देर से] हूं?

TALKING ABOUT YOURSELF

76. What is your name?
aap kaa naam kyaa hai? आप का नाम क्या है?

77. I am Mr. [Talvar].
main [tal-vaar] saa-hab hoon. मै॰ [तलवार साहब] हूं।

78. My name is [John].
mé-raa naam [jaan] hai. मेरा नाम [जान] है।

79. I am [21] years old.
main [ik-kees] saal kaa hoon. मै॰ [इक्कीस] साल का हूं।

80. I am [an American citizen].
main [am-re-kee naag-rik] hoon. मै॰ [अमरीकी नागरिक] हूं।

81. My address is [352 Tulsidas Street].
mé-raa pa-taa [teen sau baa-van tul-see-daas maarg] hai. मेरा पता [३५२ तुलसीदास मार्ग] है।

82. I am [a student].
main [vi-dhyaar-thee] hoon. मै॰ [विद्यार्थी] हूं।

83. —a teacher.
—a-dhyaa-pak. _ अध्यापक।

84. —a businessman.
—vyav-saa-yee. _ व्यवसायी।

85. —a trader.
—vyaa-paa-ree. _ व्यापारी।

86. What is your job?

aap kaa kaam kyaa hai? आप का काम क्या है?

87. I am a friend [of Ravi].

main [ra-vee] [kaa dost (M.)] [kee sa-hé-lee (F.)] hoon.

मैं [रवी] [का दोस्त] [की सहेली] हूं।

88. He works for [Hindustan Lever].

vo [hin-du-staan lee-var] ké li-yé kaam kar-taa hai.

वह [हिन्दुस्तान लीवर] के लिये काम करता है।

89. I am here [on a vacation].

main ya-haan [chhuT-Tee par] hoon.

मैं यहां [छुट्टी पर] हूं।

90. —on a business trip.

—kaam sé [aa-yaa (M.)] [aa-ee (F.)]. _ काम से [आया] [आई]।

91. I have been here [one week].

main ya-haan [ék haf-té] sé hoon.

मैं यहां [एक हफ्ते] से हूं।

92. We plan to stay here until [Friday].

[shu-kra-vaar] tak réh-né kee ich-chhaa hai.

[शुक्रवार] तक रहने की इच्छा है।

93. I am traveling to [Benaras].

main [vaa-raa-na-see] jaa [ra-haa (M.)] [ra-hee (F.)] hoon.

मैं [वारानसी] जा [रहा] [रही] हूं।

94. I am in a hurry.

main jal-dee mén hoon.   मैं जल्दी में हूं।

95. I feel [cold] [warm].

mu-jhé [THanD] [gar-mee] lag ra-hee hai.

मुझे [ठंड] [गर्मी] लग रही है।

96. I am [hungry] [thirsty].
mu-jhé [bhook] [pyaas] la-gee hai.
मुझे [भूक] [प्यास] लगी है।

97. I am busy.
mu-jhé ba-hut kaam hai.
मुझे बहुत काम है।

98. I am tired.
main thak [ga-yaa (M.)] [ga-ee (F.)] hoon.
मैं थक [गया] [गई] हूँ।

99. I am glad (OR: **happy**).
main *khush* (OR: pra-sann) hoon.   मैं खुश (प्रसन्न) हूँ।

100. I am disappointed.
mu-jhé ni-raa-shaa hu-ee.   मुझे निराशा हुई।

101. I cannot do it.
main na-heen kar [sak-taa (M.)] [sak-tee (F.)].
मैं नहीं कर [सकता] [सकती]।

102. We are unhappy.
ham u-daas hain.   हम उदास हैं।

103. They are angry.
vé *ghus*-sé hain.   वे गुस्से हैं।

MAKING YOURSELF UNDERSTOOD

104. Do you speak [English]?
kyaa aap [an-gré-zee] bol [lé-té (M.)] [lé-tee (F.)] hain?
क्या आप [अँग्रेज़ी] बोल [लेते][लेती] हैं?

105. Where is [English] spoken?

[an-gré-zee] ka-haan bo-lee jaa-tee hai?

[अंग्रेज़ी] कहाँ बोली जाती है?

106. Does anyone here speak [French]?

kyaa ya-haan ko-ee [fraan-see-see bhaa-shaa] bol sak-taa hai?

क्या यहाँ कोई [फ़्रांसीसी भाषा] बोल सकता है?

107. I read only [Italian].

main ké-val [i-Tai-li-yan] paRH [sak-taa (M.)] [sak-tee (F.)] hoon.

मैं केवल [इटैलियन] पढ़ [सकता] [सकती] हूँ।

108. I speak a little [German].

main kuchh [jar-man] bol [lé-taa (M.)] [lé-tee (F.)] hoon.

मैं कुछ जर्मन बोल [लेता] [लेती] हूँ।

109. Speak more slowly.

za-raa dhee-ré bo-li-yé. ज़रा धीरे बोलिये।

110. I [do not] understand.

main [na-heen] [sam-jhaa (M.)] [sam-jhee (F.)].

मैं [नहीं] [समझा] [समझी]।

111. Do you understand me?

aap né mé-ree baat sam-jhee? आप ने मेरी बात समझी?

112. I [do not] know.

mu-jhé pa-taa [na-heen] hai. मुझे पता [नहीं] है।

113. I think so.

mé-raa vi-chaar hai. मेरा विचार है।

114. Repeat it.

phir sé bo-li-yé. फिर से बोलिये।

115. Write it down.
likh dee-ji-yé. लिख दीजिये ।

116. Answer "yes" or "no."
"haan" yaa "naa" ka-hi-yé. "हाँ" या "ना" कहिये ।

117. You are right.
aap THeek [kéh-té (M.)] [kéh-tee (F.)] hain.
आप ठीक [कहते] [कहती] हैं ।

118. That is wrong.
yé gha-lat hai. यह ग़लत है ।

119. What is the meaning of [this word]?
[is shabd] kaa kyaa arth hai?
[इस शब्द] का क्या अर्थ है?

120. How do you say ["pencil"] in [Hindi]?
hin-dee mén [pain-sil] ko kyaa kéh-té hain?
हिन्दी में ["पैनसिल"] को क्या कहते हैं?

121. How do you spell ["Simla"]?
[sim-laa] kai-sé likh-té hain? ["सिमला"] कैसे लिखते हैं?

DIFFICULTIES &
MISUNDERSTANDINGS

122. Where is [the American Embassy]?
[am-ree-kan ém-bai-see] ka-haan hai?
[अमरीकन एमबैसी] कहाँ है?

123. —the police station.
—thaa-naa. _ थाना ।

124. —the enquiry office.

—poochh-taachh kaa daf-tar. _ पूछ-ताछ का दफ़्तर।

125. I want to see [your superior].

main [aap ké af-sar] sé mil-naa [chaa-ha-taa (M.)] [chaa-
ha-tee (F.)] hoon.

मै॰ [आप के अफ़्सर] से मिलना [चाहता] [चाहती] हूँ।

126. Can you [help] me?

kyaa aap mé-ree [sa-haa-ya-taa kar] [sak-té (M.)] [sak-tee
(F.)] hain?

क्या आप मेरी [सहायता कर] [सकते] [सकती] है॰?

127. Can you tell me how to get there?

kyaa aap ba-taa [sak-té (M.)] [sak-tee (F.)] hain ki main
va-haan kai-sé jaa-oon?

क्या आप बता [सकते] [सकती] है॰ कि मै॰ वहाँ कैसे जाऊं?

128. I am looking for [my friend].

main [ap-né mi-tra (M.)] [ap-nee sa-hé-lee (F.)] ko
DHoonDH [ra-haa (M.)] [ra-hee (F.)] hoon.

मै॰ [अपने मित्र] [अपनी सहेली] को ढूँढ [रहा] [रही] हूँ।

129. I am lost.

main raas-taa bhool [ga-yaa (M.)] [ga-ee (F.)] hoon.

मै॰ रास्ता भूल [गया] [गई] हूँ।

130. I cannot find [the address].

mu-jhé [pa-taa] na-heen mil ra-haa.

मुझे [पता] नहीं मिल रहा।

131. She has lost [her handbag].

[in kaa ba-Tu-aa] kho ga-yaa hai. [इन का बटुआ] खो
गया है।

132. We forgot [our keys].

ham [ap-nee chaa-bee] bhool aa-yé.

हम [अपनी चाबी] भूल आये।

133. We missed [the train].

ha-maa-ree [gaa-Ree] chhooT ga-ee.

हमारी [गाड़ी] छूट गई ।

134. It is not my [fault].

yé mé-ree [ghal-tee] na-heen.

यह [मेरी गलती] नहीं ।

135. I do [not] remember [the name].

mu-jhé [naam] yaad [na-heen] hai.

मुझे [नाम] याद [नहीं] है ।

136. Don't bother us (OR: **Let us alone)!**

ha-mén tang mat ka-ro (OR: ha-mén réh-né do)!

हमें तंग मत करो (हमें रहने दो) ।

137. Go away!

bhaag jaa-o (OR: cha-lé jaa-o)!

भाग जाओ (चले जाओ) ।

138. Help!

ba-chaa-o!   बचाओ ।

139. Police!

pu-lis!   पुलिस ।

140. Thief!

chor!   चोर ।

141. Fire!

aag!   आग ।

142. Look out!

ba-cho!   बचो ।

143. This is an emergency.

yé khat-ré kaa ai-laan hai.   यह ख़तरे का ऐलान है ।

144. This is urgent.
yé ba-hut za-roo-ree hai.   यह बहुत ज़रूरी है।

CUSTOMS

145. Where is [the customs office]?
[chun-gee kaa daf-tar] ka-haan hai?
[चुंगी का दफ़्तर] कहाँ है?

146. Here is [our baggage].
yé [ha-maa-raa saa-maan] hai.   यह [हमारा सामान] है।

147. —my passport.
—mé-raa paas-porT. _ मेरा पासपोर्ट।

148. —my identification card.
—mé-raa pa-ri-chay pa-tra. _ मेरा परिचय पत्र।

149. —my health certificate.
—mé-ré svaasth-ya kaa pra-maaN-pa-tra.
_ मेरे स्वास्थ्य का प्रमाण पत्र।

150. —my visitor's visa.
—mé-raa Too-risT vee-zaa. _ मेरा टूरिस्ट वीज़ा।

151. I am in transit.
main sa-far mén hoon.   मैं॰ सफ़र में हूँ।

152. [The bags] over there are mine.
jo u-dhar ra-khaa hai [vo saa-maan] mé-raa hai.
जो उधर रखा है [वह सामान] मेरा है।

153. Must I open everything?
kyaa sab khol-naa pa-Ré-gaa?   क्या सब खोलना पड़ेगा?

154. I cannot open [the trunk].
mujh sé [yé ba-kas] na-heen khul ra-haa.
मुझ से [यह बकस] नहीं खुल रहा।

155. There is nothing here [but clothing].

is mén [kap-Ron ké si-vaa] kuchh na-heen.

इस में [कपड़ों के सिवा] कुछ नहीं ।

156. I have nothing to declare.

mé-ré paas chun-gee vaa-laa ko-ee saa-maan na-heen hai.

मेरे पास चुंगी वाला कोई सामान नहीं है ।

157. Everything is for my personal use.

yé mé-ré ap-né is-té-maal ké li-yé hai.

यह मेरे अपने इस्तेमाल के लिये है ।

158. I bought [this necklace] in [America].

[yé haar] main né [am-ree-kaa] mén kha-ree-daa thaa.

[यह हार] मैं ने [अमरीका] में खरीदा था ।

159. These are [gifts].

yé [to-fé] hain.   ये [तोहफ़े] हैं ।

160. This is all I have.

bas mé-ré paas ya-hee hai. बस मेरे पास यही है ।

161. Must duty be paid on [these things]?

kyaa [in chee-zon] par chun-gee la-gé-gee?

क्या [इन चीज़ों] पर चुंगी लगेगी?

162. Have you finished?

kyaa kaam poo-raa ho ga-yaa? क्या काम पूरा हो गया?

BAGGAGE

163. Where can we check our luggage through to [Agra]?

ham ap-naa saa-maan see-dhaa [aa-graa] ka-haan sé bhéj sak-té hain?

हम अपना सामान सीधा [आगरा] कहाँ से भेज सकते हैं?

164. These things to the [left] [right] belong to me.

yé [baa-én haath] [daa-hi-né haath] vaa-lee chee-zén mé-
ree hain.

यह [बाएं हाथ] [दहिने हाथ] वाली चीज़ें मेरी हैं।

165. I cannot find all my baggage.

mu-jhé ap-naa poo-raa saa-maan na-heen mil ra-haa hai.

मुझे अपना पूरा सामान नहीं मिल रहा।

166. One of my [packages] is missing.

mé-ree ék [poT-lee] kam hai.   मेरी एक [पोटली] कम है।

167. I want to leave [this suitcase] here [for a few days].

main [is ba-kas] ko [kuchh di-non ké li-yé] ya-haan
chhoR-naa [chaa-ha-taa (M.)] [chaa-ha-tee (F.)] hoon.

मैं [इस बकस] को [कुछ दिनों के लिये] यहाँ छोड़ना
[चाहता] [चाहती] हूँ।

168. Give me [a receipt] for the baggage.

saa-maan ké li-yé mu-jhé [ra-seed] dee-ji-yé.

सामान के लिये मुझे [रसीद] दीजिये।

169. I own [a black trunk].

mé-ré paas [kaa-laa ba-kas] hai.

मेरे पास [काला बकस] है।

170. I have four pieces of luggage altogether.

mé-ré paas kul chaar a-dat saa-maan hai.

मेरे पास कुल चार अदत सामान है।

171. Carry this to the baggage room.

i-sé as-baab ghar lé cha-lo.   इसे असबाब घर ले चलो!

172. Don't forget that.

u-sé na-heen bhool-naa.   उसे नहीं भूलना।

173. I shall carry this myself.

ma͞in i-sé sva-yam lé [jaa-o͞on-gaa (M.)] [jaa-o͞on-gee (F.)].

मैं इसे स्वयम ले [जाऊंगा] [जाऊंगी]।

174. Follow me.

mé-ré pee-chhé cha-li-yé.   मेरे पीछे चलिये।

175. Come with me.

mé-ré saath cha-li-yé.   मेरे साथ चलिये।

176. I would like [a taxi] [a porter].

mu-jhé [Taik-see] [ku-lee] chaa-hi-yé.

मुझे [टैक्सी] [कुली] चाहिये।

177. This is very fragile.

yé ba-hut jal-dee TooT sak-taa hai.

यह बहुत जल्दी टूट सकता है।

178. Handle this carefully.

i-sé sam-bhaal kar u-THaa-i-yé.

इसे सम्भाल कर उठाइये।

179. How much do I owe you?

mu-jhé aap ko kit-né pai-sé dé-né ha͞in?

मुझे आप को कितने पैसे देने हैं?

180. What is the customary tip?

ya-haa͞n kit-nee ba*kh*-shish dee jaa-tee hai?

यहाँ कितनी बख़्शिश दी जाती है?

TRAVEL DIRECTIONS

181. I want to go [to the airline office].

ma͞in [ha-vaa-ee ja-haaz ké daf-tar] jaa-naa [chaa-ha-taa (M.)] [chaa-ha-tee (F.)] ho͞on.

मैं [हवाई जहाज़ के दफ़्तर] जाना [चाहता] [चाहती] हूँ।

182. —to the travel agent's office.

—Trai-val ai-jénT ké daf-tar. _ ट्रैवल ऐजेन्ट के दफ़्तर ।

183. —to the government tourist office.

—sar-kaa-ree Too-risT daf-tar.

_ सरकारी टूरिस्ट दफ़्तर ।

184. How long does it take to walk [to the Red Fort]?

[laal ki-lé] pai-dal jaa-né men kit-nee dér la-gé-gee?

[लाल किले] पैदल जाने में कितनी देर लोगी?

185. Is this the shortest way to [the Jama Mosque]?

kyaa [ja-maa mas-jid] jaa-né kaa yé sab sé see-dhaa raas-
taa hai?

क्या [जमा मसजिद] जाने का यह सब से सीधा रास्ता
है?

**186. Show me the way to [the center of town] [the shop-
ping section].**

[sha-hér ké beech] [baa-zaar] jaa-né kaa raas-taa ba-taa-
i-yé.

[शहर के बीच] [बाज़ार] जाने का रास्ता बताइये ।

**187. Do I turn to [the north] [the south] [the east] [the
west]?**

kyaa main [ut-tar] [da-kshiN] [poo-rav] [pash-chim] kee
ta-raf jaa-oon?

क्या मै॰ [उत्तर] [दक्षिण] [पूरव] [पश्चिम] जाऊं?

188. [Which street] is this?

yé [kaun-see sa-Rak] hai? यह [कौनसी सड़क] है?

189. How far is it from here?

ya-haan sé kit-nee door hai? यहाँ से कितनी दूर है?

190. Is it near or far?

vo paas hai ki door? वह पास है कि दूर?

191. Can we walk there?

kyaa ham va-haan tak pai-dal jaa sak-té hain?

क्या हम वहाँ तक पैदल जा सकते है ं?

192. Am I going in the right direction?

kyaa main sa-hee di-shaa men jaa [ra-haa (M.)] [ra-hee (F.)] hoon?

क्या मै ं सही दिशा मै ं जा [रहा] [रही] हूँ ?

193. Please point.

mé-hér-baa-nee kar-ké ba-taa-i-yé.

मेहरबानी करके बताइमे ।

194. Should I go [this way] [that way]?

kyaa main [is ta-raf] [us ta-raf] ja-oon?

क्या मै ं [इस तरफ़] [उस तरफ़] जाऊँ?

195. Turn [left] [right] at the next corner.

ag-lé ko-né par [baa-én ta-raf] [daa-én ta-raf] mor lén.

आगले कोने पर [बाएँ तरफ़] [दाएँ तरफ़] मोड़ लें।

196. Is it [on this side of the street]?

kyaa vo [sa-Rak kee is ta-raf] hai?

क्या वह [सड़क की इस तरफ़] है?

197. —on the other side of the street.

—sa-Rak kee doos-ree ta-raf. _ सड़क की दूसरी तरफ़।

198. —across the bridge.

—pul ké paar. _ पुल के पार।

199. —along the boulevard.

—chau-Ree sa-Rak ké ki-naa-ré.

_ चौड़ी सड़क के किनारे।

200. —between these avenues.

—in saR-kon ké beech men. _ इन सड़कों के बीच में।

201. —beyond the traffic light.
—laal bat-tee ké aa-gé.   लाल बत्ती के आगे।

202. —next to the apartment house.
—flai-Ton vaa-lee man-zil ké paas.
  फ़्लैटों वाली मन्ज़िल के पास।

203. —in the middle of the block.
—blaak ké bee-cho-beech.   ब्लाक के बीचोबीच।

204. —straight ahead.
—see-dhaa aa-gé.   सीधा आगे।

205. —inside the station.
—i-sTé-shan ké an-dar.   इस्टेशन के अन्दर।

206. —near the square.
—chauk ké paas.   चौक के पास।

207. —outside the lobby.
—laa-bee ké baa-har.   लाबी के बाहर।

208. —at the entrance.
—phaa-Tak (OR: pra-vésh) par.   फाटक (प्रवेश) पर।

209. —opposite the park.
—paark (OR: baa-gee-ché) ké saam-né.   पार्क (बागिचे)
                         के सामने।

210. —beside the school.
—i-skool ké ba-*ghal* mén.   इस्कूल के बग़ल में।

211. —in front of the monument.
—smaa-rak ké saam-né.   स्मारक के सामने।

212. —in the rear of the store.
—du-kaan kee pichh-lee ta-raf.
  दुकान की पिछली तरफ़।

213. —behind the building.
—man-zil ké pee-chhé. _ मन्ज़िल के पीछे।

214. —up the hill.
—pa-haa-Ree ké oo-par. _ पहाड़ी के ऊपर।

215. —down the stairs.
—see-RHi-yon̄ ké nee-ché. _ सीढ़ियों के नीचे।

216. —around the traffic circle.
—gol-chak-kar sé ho kar. _ गोलचक्कर से हो कर।

217. The factory.
kaar-*kh*aa-naa. कारख़ाना।

218. The office building.
daf-tar kaa bha-van. दफ़्तर का भवन।

219. The residential section.
aa-vaa-see-ya kshé-tra. आवासीय क्षेत्र।

220. The suburbs.
kaa-lo-nee. कालोनी।

221. The city.
sha-hér (OR: na-gar). शहर (नगर)।

222. The countryside.
dé-haat. देहात।

223. The village.
gaa-on̄. गाँव।

224. The district.
zi-laa. ज़िला।

BOAT

225. When must I go on board?
mu-jhé ja-haaz par kab chaRH-naa pa-Ré-gaa?
मुझे जहाज़ पर कब चढ़ना पड़ेगा?

226. I want to rent a deck chair.
mu-jhé ki-raa-yé par kur-see lé-nee chaa-hi-yé.
मुझे किराये पर कुर्सी लेनी चाहिये।

227. Can we go ashore at [Cochin]?
kyaa ham [ko-chin] mén u-tar sak-té hain?
क्या हम [कोचिन] में उतर सकते हैं?

228. At what time is dinner served?
raat kaa khaa-naa kab khaa-yaa jaa-taa hai?
रात का खाना कब खाया जाता है?

229. When is the [first sitting] [the second sitting]?
[péh-lee bai-THak] [doos-ree bai-THak] kab hai?
[पहली बैठक] [दूसरी बैठक] कब है?

230. I feel seasick.
mu-jhé mat-lee ho ra-hee hai. मुझे मतली हो रही है।

231. Have you a remedy for seasickness?
kyaa aap ké paas mat-lee rok-né kee da-vaa hai?
क्या आप के पास मतली रोकने की दवा है?

232. Lifeboat.
ra-kshaa-nau-kaa. रक्षा-नौका।

233. Life preserver.
praaN-ra-kshak. प्राणरक्षक।

234. The ferry.
naa-o. नाव।

235. The dock.
ban-dar (OR: ghaaT). बन्दर (घाट) ।

236. The cabin.
kai-bin (OR: da-boo-saa). कैबिन (दबूसा) ।

237. The deck.
ta*kh*-taa. तख़्तT ।

238. The gymnasium.
vyaa-yaam-shaa-laa. व्यायामशाला ।

239. The swimming pool.
tair-né kaa taa-laab. तैरने का तालाब ।

240. The captain.
kap-taan. कप्तान ।

241. The purser.
ja-haaz kaa *kha*-zaan-chee (OR: par-sar).
जहाज़ का ख़ज़ाँची (पर्सर) ।

242. The cabin steward.
kai-bin bai-raa. कैबिन बैरT ।

243. The dining-room steward.
i-sToo-arD saa-hab. इस्ट्अर्ड साहब ।

AIRPLANE*

244. I want [to make] [to cancel] a reservation.
mu-jhé ré-zar-vé-shan [kar-vaa-naa] [radd kar-vaa-naa]
hai.
मुझे रेज़रवेश्न [करवाना] [रद्द करवाना] है ।

* Official airline usage contains many English terms.

245. When is the next flight to [Calcutta]?

[kal-kat-té] jaa-né vaa-lee ag-lee u-Raan kab hai?

[कलकत्ते] जाने वाली आगली उड़ान कब है?

246. When does the plane arrive at [Madras]?

vi-maan [mad-raas] kab pa-hun-ché-gaa?

विमान [मदरास] कब पहुँचेगा?

247. What kind of plane is used on this flight?

is sa-far men̐ kaun-sé vi-maan kaa is-té-maal ho-gaa?

इस सफ़र में कौनसे विमान का इस्तेमाल होगा?

248. Will food be served?

kyaa khaa-naa mi-lé-gaa? क्या खाना मिलेगा?

249. May I confirm the reservation by telephone?

kyaa main Té-lee-fon par ré-zar-vé-shan pak-kee kar-vaa [sak-taa (M.)] [sak-tee (F.)] hoon?

क्या मैं टेलीफोन पर रेज़रवेशन पक्की करवा [सकता] [सकती] हूँ?

250. At what time should we check in [at the airport]?

ham [ha-vaa-ee aD-Dé] kis sa-may pa-hun-chen̐?

हम [हवाई अड्डे] किस समय पहुँचें?

251. How long does it take to get to the airport from my hotel?

ho-Tal sé ha-vaa-ee aD-Dé pa-hunch-né men̐ kit-nee dér lag-tee hai?

होटल से हवाई अड्डे पहुँचने में कितनी देर लगती है?

252. Is there bus service between the airport and the city?

kyaa ha-vaa-ee aD-Dé aur sha-hér ké beech bas chal-tee hai?

क्या हवाई अड्डे और शहर के बीच बस चलती है?

253. Is that flight [nonstop] [direct]?
kyaa vi-maan [bi-naa ru-ké] [see-dhé] jaa-yé-gaa?
क्या विमान [बिना रुके] [सीधे] जायेगा?

254. Where does the plane stop en route?
vi-maan ka-haan sé ho-té hu-é jaa-yé-gaa?
विमान कहाँ से होते हुए जायेगा?

255. How long do we stop?
kit-nee dér tak ru-ké-gaa? कितनी देर तक रुकेगा?

256. May I stop over in [Hyderabad]?
kyaa main raas-té men [hai-da-raa-baad] THa-hér [sak-
taa (M.)] [sak-tee (F.)] hoon?
क्या मैं रास्ते में [हैदराबाद] ठहर [सकता] [सकती]
हूँ?

257. We want to travel [first class] [economy class].
ham [farsT klaas] [Too-risT klaas] men sa-far kar-naa
chaa-ha-té hain.
हम [फ़र्स्ट क्लास] [टूरिस्ट क्लास] में सफ़र करना चाहते
हैं।

258. Is flight [number 22] on time?
kyaa [baa-ees nam-bar] u-Raan sa-may par hai?
क्या [बाईस नम्बर] उड़ान समय पर है?

259. How much baggage am I allowed?
kit-naa saa-maan lé jaa-naa THeek hai?
कितना सामान ले जाना ठीक है?

260. How much per kilo for excess baggage?
a-dhik saa-maan ké pra-ti ki-lo kaa kyaa réT hai?
अधिक सामान के प्रति किलो का क्या रेट है?

261. May I carry this on board?

kyaa main i-sé vi-maan ké an-dar lé jaa [sak-taa (M.)] [sak-tee (F.)] hoon?

क्या मैं॑ इसे विमान के अन्दर ले जा [सकता] [सकती] हूँ?

262. Give me a seat [on the aisle].

mu-jhé [ga-li-yaa-ré ké ba-*ghal* vaa-lee] ja-gah dén.

मुझे [गलियारे के बगल वाली] जगह दें।

263. —by a window.

—khiR-kee ké paas. _ खिड़की के पास।

264. —by the emergency exit.

—aa-paa-tee dvaar ké paas. _ आपाती द्वार के पास।

265. May we board the plane now?

kyaa ab ham vi-maan mén chaRH sak-té hain?

क्या अब हम विमान में चढ़ सकते है॑?

266. From which gate does my flight leave?

mé-raa vi-maan kis géT sé jaa-taa hai?

मेरा विमान किस गेट से जाता है?

267. Call the stewardess.

é-yar hos-Tés ko bu-laa-i-yé. एयर होस्टेस को बुलाइये।

268. Fasten your seat belt.

seeT kee pé-Tee baan-dhi-yé. सीट की पेटी बांधिये।

269. May I smoke?

kyaa main dhu-mar-paan kar [sak-taa (M.)] [sak-tee (F.)] hoon?

क्या मैं॑ धुम्रपान कर [सकता] [सकती] हूँ?

270. Will we arrive [on time] [late]?

kyaa ham [sa-may par] [dér mén] pa-hun-chén-gé?

क्या हम [समय पर] [देर मैं] पहुँचेंगे?

271. An announcement.
sooch-naa. सूचना।

272. A boarding pass.
vi-maan pa-tra. विमान पत्र।

TRAIN

273. When does the ticket office [open] [close]?
Ti-kaT-ghar kab [khu-lé-gaa] [band ho-gaa]?
टिकट-घर कब [खुलेगा] [बन्द होगा]?

274. When does the next train for [Jodhpur] leave?
[jodh-pur] jaa-né vaa-lee ag-lee gaa-Ree kab chhoo-Té-gee?
[जोधपुर] जाने वाली आगली गाड़ी कब छूटेगी?

275. Is there [an earlier train] [a later train]?
kyaa us ké [péh-lé ko-ee gaa-Ree] [baad ko-ee gaa-Ree]
jaa-tee hai?
क्या उस के [पहले कोई गाड़ी][बाद कोई गाड़ी] जाती है?

276. When does the [express] [local] train leave?
[éks-prés] [pai-sin-jar] gaa-Ree kab chhooT-tee hai?
[एक्सप्रेस] [पैसिंजर] गाड़ी कब छूटती है?

277. From which platform does the train leave?
gaa-Ree kis plaiT-faarm sé chhooT-tee hai?
गाड़ी किस प्लेट्फ़ार्म से छूटती है?

278. Where can I get a timetable?
sa-may-soo-chee ka-haan mil-tee hai?
समय-सूची कहाँ मिलती है?

279. Does this train stop at [Poona]?
kyaa yé gaa-Ree [poo-né] ruk-tee hai?
क्या यह गाड़ी [पूने] रुकती है?

280. Is there time to get off?

kyaa u-tar-né ké li-yé sa-may ho-gaa?

क्या उतरने के लिये समय होगा?

281. When do we arrive?

ham kab pa-hun-chén-gé? हम कब पहुँचेंगे?

282. Is this seat empty?

kyaa yé ja-gah *khaa*-lee hai? क्या यह जगह खाली है?

283. Am I disturbing you?

main aap ko pa-ré-shaan to na-heen kar [ra-haa (M.)] [ra-hee (F.)] hoon?

मैं आप को परेशान तो नहीं कर [रहा] [रही] हूं?

284. Open the window.

khiR-kee khol dee-ji-yé. खिड़की खोल दीजिये।

285. Close the door.

dar-vaa-zaa band kee-ji-yé. दरवाज़ा बन्द कीजिये।

286. Where are we now?

ab ham ka-haan hain? अब हम कहाँ हैं?

287. Is the train on time?

kyaa gaa-Ree sa-may par hai? क्या गाड़ी समय पर है?

288. How late are we?

gaa-Ree kit-nee dér sé chal ra-hee hai?

गाड़ी कितनी देर से चल रही है?

289. The conductor.

Ti-kaT ka-lék-Tar (OR: kan-Dak-Tar saa-hab).

टिकट कलेक्टर (कन्डकटर साहब)।

290. The gate.

phaa-Tak. फाटक।

291. The information office (OR: booth).
poochh-taachh daf-tar.   पूछ-ताछ दफ़्तर ।

292. A one-way ticket.
ék ta-raf kaa Ti-kaT.   एक तरफ़ का टिकट ।

293. A round-trip ticket.
ri-Tarn Ti-kaT.   रिटर्न टिकट ।

294. A platform ticket.
plaiT-faarm Ti-kaT.   प्लैट्फ़ार्म टिकट ।

295. The railroad station.
rél-vé i-sTé-shan.   रेलवे इस्टेशन ।

296. The waiting room.
pra-tee-kshaa-lay.   प्रतीक्षालय ।

297. The sleeping car.
shay-ni-kaa.   शयनिका ।

298. The first class bedroom compartment for two.
koo-pé.   कूपे ।

299. The smoking car.
dhu-mar-paan Dib-baa.   धुम्रपान डिब्बा ।

300. The dining car.
bho-jan-yaan.   भोजनालय ।

301. The compartment.
Dib-baa.   डिब्बा ।

302. The ladies' compartment.
ma-hi-laa (OR: za-naa-naa) Dib-baa.
महिला (ज़नाना) डिब्बा ।

BUS AND STREETCAR

303. Where does [the streetcar] stop?
[Traam] ka-haan ruk-tee hai?   [ट्राम] कहाँ रुकती है?

304. How often does [the bus] run?
[bas] kit-nee baar chal-tee hai?
[बस] कितनी बार चलती है?

305. Which bus goes to [Jaipur]?
[jai-pur] kaun-see bas jaa-tee hai?
[जैपुर] कौनसी बस जाती है?

306. How much is the fare?
ki-raa-yaa kit-naa hai?   किरायमा कितना है?

307. Do you pass by [Shanti Path]?
kyaa aap [shaan-tee path] ké paas sé gu-zar-té hain?
क्या आप [शान्ती पथ] के पास से गुज़रते हैं?

308. I want to get off [at the next stop] [right here].
main [ag-lé THa-hé-raa-o par] [ya-heen par] u-tar-naa
   [chaa-ha-taa (M.)] [chaa-ha-tee (F.)] hoon.
मैं [आगले ठहराव पर] [यही पर] उतरना [चाहता]
[चाहती] हूँ।

309. Please tell me where to get off.
mu-jhé ba-taa-i-yé ki main ka-haan ut-roon.
मुझे बताइये कि मैं कहाँ उतरूँ।

310. Will I have to change buses?
kyaa mu-jhé bas ba-dal-nee pa-Ré-gee?
क्या मुझे बस बदलनी पड़ेगी?

311. Where do we transfer?
ham bas ka-haan bad-len?   हम बस कहाँ बदलें?

312. The driver.
Draa-i-var saa-hab.   ड्राइवर साहब।

313. The bus stop.

bas aD-Daa (OR: bas i-sTaap).

बस अड्डा (बस इस्टाप) ।

TAXI AND RICKSHAW

314. Where can I get a (scooter) rickshaw?

(i-skoo-Tar) rik-shaa ka-haan mi-lé-gee?

(इस्कूटर) रिक्शा कहाँ मिलेगी?

315. Call a taxi for me.

Taik-see mang-vaa dee-ji-yé.   टैक्सी मँगवा दीजिये।

316. Are you free, driver?

kyaa aap kee gaa-Ree *khaa*-lee hai?

क्या आप की गाड़ी खाली है?

317. What do you charge [per hour]?

aap [pra-ti ghan-Té] kyaa lé-té hain?

आप [प्रति घन्टे] क्या लेते हैं?

318. —per kilometer.

—pra-ti ki-lo-mee-Tar.   _प्रति किलोमीटर।

319. —per day.

—pra-ti din. _ प्रति दिन।

320. Take me to this address.

mu-jhé is pa-té par lé cha-li-yé.

मुझे इस पते पर ले चलिये।

321. How much will the ride cost?

sa-vaa-ree ké kit-né pai-sé la-gén-gé?

सवारी के कितने पैसे लगेंगे?

322. How long will it take to get there?
pa-hunch-né men kit-nee dér la-gé-gee?
पहुंचने में कितनी देर लगेगी?

323. Drive us around [for one hour].
ha-mén [ék ghan-Té bhar] ghu-maa-i-yé.
हमें [एक घन्टे भर] घुमाइये।

324. Drive more carefully.
dhyaan sé cha-laa-i-yé. ध्यान से चलाइये।

325. Drive more slowly.
za-raa dhee-ré cha-laa-i-yé. ज़रा धीरे चलाइये।

326. I am [not] in a great hurry.
main jal-dee mén [na-heen] hoon.
मैं जल्दी में [नहीं] हूं।

327. Stop here.
ya-haan ru-ki-yé. यहां रुकिये।

328. Wait for me here.
mé-ré li-yé ya-haan THa-hé-ri-yé.
मेरे लिये यहां ठहरिये।

329. I will return in [five minutes].
main [paanch mi-naT] mén [lau-Toon-gaa (M.)] [lau-
Toon-gee (F.)].
मैं [पांच मिनट] में [लौटूंगा] [लौटूंगी]।

330. Keep the change.
baa-qee aap ra-khén. बाक़ी आप रखें।

331. The taxi stand.
Taik-see aD-Daa. टैक्सी अड्डा।

332. The taxi meter.
mee-Tar. मीटर।

RENTING AUTOS

333. What kind of [cars] do you have? ___
aap ké paas kaun-see [mo-Tar gaa-Ri-yaan] hain?

आप के पास कौनसी [मोटर गाड़ियाँ] है ँ?

334. I have an international driver's license.
mé-ré paas in-Tar-naish-nal Draa-i-ving laa-ee-séns hai.

मेरे पास इन्टरनैशनल ड्राइविंग लाइसेन्स है।

335. What is the rate [per day]?
[pra-ti din] ka kyaa ki-raa-yaa hai?

[प्रति दिन] का क्या किरामा है?

336. How much additional [per kilometer]? ___
[har ki-lo-mee-Tar] ké kit-né pai-sé aur lag-té hain?

[हर किलोमीटर] के कितने पैसे और लगते है ँ?

337. Are expenses for gas and oil also included?
kyaa us mén pé-Trol aur tél kaa *kh*arch bhee joR li-yaa hai?

क्या उस मैं पेट्रोल और तेल का ख़र्च भी जोड़ लिया है?

338. Does the insurance policy cover [personal liability]?
kyaa bee-mé mén [ha-maa-ree zim-mé-vaa-ree] kaa pra-bandh hai?

क्या बीमे मैं [हमारी ज़िम्मेवारी] का प्रबन्ध है?

339. —property damage.
—nuq-saan kee zim-mé-vaa-ree.

_ नुक़्सान की ज़िम्मेवारी।

340. —collision.
—Tak-kar kee zim-mé-vaa-ree. _ टक्कर की ज़िम्मेवारी।

341. Are the papers in order?

kyaa laa-ec-séns va-ghai-rah THeek hain?

क्या लाईसेन्स वगैरह ठीक है'?

342. I am not familiar with this car.

mu-jhé is gaa-Ree kaa a-nu-bhav na-heen hai.

मुझे इस गाड़ी का अनुभव नहीं है।

343. Explain this [dial] [mechanism].

yé [mee-Tar] [yan-tra] mu-jhé sam-jhaa-i-yé.

यह [मीटर] [यंत्र] मुझे समझाइये।

344. How does [the heater] operate?

[taa-pak] kai-sé chal-taa hai? [तापक] कैसे चलता है?

345. Will someone pick it up at the hotel?

kyaa ho-Tal sé i-sé ko-ee lé-né aa-yé-gaa?

क्या होटल से इसे कोई लेने आयेगा?

346. Is the office open [all night] [24 hours]?

kyaa daf-tar [poo-ree raat] [chau-bees ghan-Té] khu-laa
réh-taa hai?

क्या दफ़्तर [पूरी रात] [चौबीस घन्टे] खुला रहता है?

347. The bicycle.

saa-i-kil. साइकल।

348. The motorcycle.

faT-fa-Ti-yaa (OR: mo-Tar saa-i-kil).

फ़ट्फ़टिया (मोटर साइकल)।

349. The motor scooter.

i-skoo-Tar. इस्कूटर।

350. The horse and wagon.

taan-gaa. तांगा।

351. The oxcart (OR: bullock cart).

bail gaa-Ree. बैल गाड़ी।

AUTO: DIRECTIONS

352. What is the name of [this city]?

[is sha-hér] kaa kyaa naam hai?

[इस शहर] का क्या नाम है?

353. How far [to the next town]?

[ag-laa sha-hér] kit-nee door hai?

[अगला शहर] कितनी दूर है?

354. Where does [this road] lead?

[yé sa-Rak] ka-haan jaa-tee hai?

[यह सड़क] कहाँ जाती है?

355. Are there road signs?

kyaa raas-té men chinh hain?

क्या रास्ते में चिंह है ?

356. Is the road [paved] [rough]?

kyaa sa-Rak [pak-kee] [kach-chee] hai?

क्या सड़क [पक्की] [कच्ची] है?

357. Show me the easiest way.

mu-jhé sab sé aa-saan raas-taa ba-taa-i-yé.

मुझे सब से आसान रास्ता बताइये।

358. Show it to me on this map.

mu-jhé naq-shé par di-khaa-i-yé.

मुझे नक़्शे पर दिखाइये।

359. Can I avoid heavy traffic?

kyaa main bheeR sé bach [sak-taa (M.)] [sak-tee (F.)] hoon?

क्या मैं भीड़ से बच [सकता] [सकती] हूँ?

360. Is it alright to park here [for a while]?
kyaa [kuchh dér ké li-yé] ya-h̄aan̄ gaa-Ree kha-Ree kar-naa THeek hai?

क्या [कुछ देर के लिये] यहाँ गाड़ी खड़ी करना ठीक है?

361. —overnight.
—raat bhar. _ रात भर।

362. The fork.
do-raa-haa. दोराहा।

363. The intersection.
chau-raa-haa. चौराहा।

364. The major road.
*kha*as sa-Rak. ख़ास सड़क।

365. The garage.
gi-raaj. गिराज।

366. The auto repair shop.
mo-Tar kaar-*kha*a-naa. मोटर कारख़ाना।

367. The gas station.
pé-Trol pamp. पेट्रोल पम्प।

368. The parking lot.
gaa-Ree kha-Ree kar-né kee ja-gah.
गाड़ी खड़ी करने की जगह।

369. The traffic circle.
gol-chak-kar. गोलचक्कर।

370. The traffic light.
laal bat-tee. लाल बत्ती।

371. The stop sign.

THa-hér-né kaa chinh. ठहरने का चिन्ह ।

AUTO: HELP ON THE ROAD

372. My car has broken down.

mé-ree mo-Tar bi-gaR ga-ee hai.

मेरी मोटर बिगड़ गई है ।

373. Call a [mechanic].

[mo-Tar mis-tree] ko bu-laa-i-yé.

[मोटर मिस्त्री] को बुलाइये ।

374. Help me push [the car] to the side.

[mo-Tar] ko ki-naa-ré la-gaa-né mén ma-dad dee-ji-yé.

[मोटर] को किनारे लगाने में मदद दीजिये ।

375. Push me.

dhak-kaa la-gaa-i-yé.   धक्का लगाइये ।

376. May I use your [jack]?

main aap kaa [jaik] is-té-maal kar [sak-taa (M.)] [sak-tee (F.)] hoon?

मैं आप का [जैक] इस्तेमाल कर [सकता] [सकती] हूँ?

377. Change the tire.

pa-hi-yaa ba-da-li-yé.   पहिया बदलिये ।

378. My car is stuck in [the mud] [the ditch].

mé-ree gaa-Ree [kee-chaR] [naa-lee] mén phans ga-ee hai.

मेरी गाड़ी [कीचड़] [नाली] में फँस गई है ।

379. Take me to the nearest gas station.

sab sé paas vaa-lé pé-Trol pamp par lé cha-li-yé.

सब से पास वाले पेट्रोल पम्प पर ले चलिये ।

AUTO: GAS STATION & REPAIR SHOP

380. Give me [twenty] liters of [regular] [diesel] gasoline.

mu-jhé [bees] lee-Tar [pé-Trol] [Dee-zal] dee-ji-yé.

मुझे [बीस] लीटर [पेट्रोल] [डीज़ल] दीजिये।

381. Fill it up.

Taink bhar dee-ji-yé.   टैन्क भर दीजिये।

382. Check the oil.

tél chék kee-ji-yé.   तेल चेक कीजिये।

383. Lubricate the car.

gaa-Ree kee gree-sing kee-ji-yé.   गाड़ी की ग्रीसिंग कीजिये।

384. [Light] [Medium] [Heavy] oil.

[hal-kaa] [ma-dhyam] [gaa-RHaa] in-jan kaa tél.

[हलका] [मध्यम] [गाढ़ा] इन्जन का तेल।

385. Put water in the radiator.

ré-Di-yé-Tar men paa-nee Daa-li-yé.

रेडियेटर में पानी डालिये।

386. Recharge the battery.

baiT-ree chaarj kee-ji-yé.   बैटरी चार्ज कीजिये।

387. Clean the windshield.

saam-né kaa shee-shaa saaf kee-ji-yé.

सामने का शीशा साफ़ कीजिये।

388. Adjust the brakes.

brék THeek kee-ji-yé.   ब्रेक ठीक कीजिये।

389. Check the air in the tire.
pa-hi-yé kee ha-vaa chék kee-ji-yé.

पहिये की हवा चेक कीजिये।

390. Repair the flat tire.
pank-char ba-naa dee-ji-yé.   पन्कचर बना दीजिये।

391. Could you wash it [now]?
kyaa [a-bhee] dho sak-té hain?

क्या [अभी] धो सकते हैं?

392. How long must we wait?
ha-mén kit-nee dér THa-hér-naa pa-Ré-gaa?

हमें कितनी देर ठहरना पड़ेगा?

393. The motor overheats.
in-jan ga-ram ho ja-taa hai.   इन्जन गरम हो जाता है।

394. Is it leaking from somewhere?
ka-heen choo to na-heen ra-haa?

कहीं चू तो नहीं रहा?

395. It makes noise.
yé aa-vaaz [kar-taa (M.)] [kar-tee (F.)] hai.

यह आवाज़ [करता] [करती] है।

396. The lights do not work.
bat-ti-yaan jal-tee na-heen.   बत्तियाँ जलती नहीं।

397. The car does not start.
gaa-Ree chaa-loo na-heen ho ra-hee hai.

गाड़ी चालू नहीं हो रही है।

PARTS OF THE CAR

398. Accelerator.
ék-si-lé-Tar.   एक्सिलेटर।

399. Air filter.
ha-vaa-ee jaa-lee (OR: fil-Tar). हवाई जाली (फ़िल्टर) ।

400. Alcohol.
spi-riT. स्पिरिट ।

401. Axle.
aik-sil. ऐक्सिल ।

402. Battery.
baiT-ree. बैटरी ।

403. Bolt.
péch. पेच ।

404. (Foot) Brake.
brék. ब्रेक ।

405. Hand brake.
haath kaa brék. हाथ का ब्रेक ।

406. Bumper.
bam-par. बम्पर ।

407. Carburetor.
kaar-boo-ré-Tar. कारबूरेटर ।

408. Chassis.
ché-sis. चेसिस ।

409. Choke.
chok. चोक ।

410. Clutch.
klach. क्लच ।

411. Cylinder.
si-lin-Dar. सिलिन्डर ।

412. Differential.
Dif-rén-shal. डिफ़्रेंख़ल ।

413. Directional signal.
sig-nal. सिगनल ।

414. Door.
dar-vaa-zaa. दरवाज़ा ।

415. Electrical system.
bij-lee kaa sar-kiT. बिजली का सरकिट ।

416. Engine (OR: **Motor**).
in-jan. इन्जन ।

417. Exhaust pipe.
ig-zaasT paa-ip. इगज़ास्ट पाइप ।

418. Exterior.
baa-har kaa his-saa. बाहर का हिस्सा ।

419. Fan.
pan-khaa. पन्खा ।

420. Fan belt.
fain bélT. फ़ैन बेल्ट ।

421. Fender (OR: **Mudguard**).
pank-rok. पन्करोक ।

422. Flashlight.
Taarch. टार्च ।

423. Fuel pump.
fyool pamp. फ़्यूल पम्प ।

424. Fuse.
fyooz. फ़्यूज़ ।

425. Gas tank.
pé-Trol kee Tan-kee. पेट्रोल की टन्की ।

426. Gear shift.
gi-yar bad-lee. गियर बदली ।

427. First gear.
péh-laa gi-yar. पहला गियर ।

428. Second gear.
doos-raa gi-yar. दूसरा गियर ।

429. Third gear.
tees-raa gi-yar. तीसरा गियर ।

430. Fourth gear.
Taap gi-yar. टाप गियर ।

431. Reverse gear.
ri-vars (gi-yar). रिवर्स (गियर) ।

432. Neutral gear.
nyoo-Tral. न्यूट्रल ।

433. Generator.
Daa-i-na-mo. डाइनमो ।

434. Grease.
grees. ग्रीस ।

435. Hammer.
ha-thau-Raa. हथौड़ा ।

436. Heater.
taa-pak. तापक ।

437. Hood.
bau-néT. बौनेट ।

438. Horn.
bhōn-poo. भोंपू।

439. Horsepower.
haars paa-var. हार्स पावर।

440. Ignition key.
mo-Tar kee chaa-bee. मोटर की चाबी।

441. Inner tube.
Tyoob. ट्यूब।

442. Instrument panel.
Daish borD. डैश बोर्ड।

443. License plate.
gaa-Ree kaa nam-bar. गाड़ी की नम्बर।

444. Light.
bat-tee. बत्ती।

445. Headlight.
saam-né kee bat-tee. सामने की बत्ती।

446. Brake light.
brék kee bat-tee. ब्रेक की बत्ती।

447. Taillight.
peech-lee bat-tee. पीछली बत्ती।

448. Rear-view mirror.
an-dar kaa shee-shaa. अन्दर का शीशा।

449. Side-view mirror.
ba-ghal kaa shee-shaa. बग़ल का शीशा।

450. Muffler.
saa-i-lén-sar (OR: ni-shab-dak). साइलेन्सर (निश्ब्दक)।

451. Nail.
keel. कील ।

452. Nut.
DHib-ree. ढिबरी ।

453. Pedal.
pé-Dal. पैडल ।

454. Pliers.
pi-laas. पिलास ।

455. Radiator.
ré-Di-yé-Tar. रेडियेटर ।

456. Radio.
ré-Di-yo. रेडियो ।

457. Rags.
jhaa-Ran. झाड़न ।

458. Rope.
ras-see. रस्सी ।

459. Screw.
pénch. पेंच ।

460. Screwdriver.
pénch-kas. पेंचकस ।

461. Hand shift.
gi-yar ba-dal-né vaa-lee. गियर बदलने वाली ।

462. Shock absorber.
dhak-kaa-sa-ha. धक्कासह ।

463. Spark plugs.
sphu-ling plag (OR: chin-gaa-ree plag).
स्फुलिंग प्लग (चिनगारी प्लग) ।

464. Speedometer.
chaal-maa-pee. चालमापी ।

465. Starter.
i-sTaar-Tar. इस्टार्टर ।

466. Steering wheel.
chaa-lan-chak-kaa. चालन-चक्का ।

467. Tire.
Taa-yar. टायर ।

468. Spare tire.
sTép-nee (OR: faal-too pa-hi-yaa).
स्टेपनी (फ़ालतू पहिया) ।

469. Tubeless tire.
bi-naa Tyoob kaa Taa-yar. बिना टमूब का टायर ।

470. Tire pump.
ha-vaa bhar-né vaa-laa. हवा भरने वाला ।

471. Tools.
au-zaar. औज़ार ।

472. Trunk.
Dik-kee (OR: booT). डिक्की (बूट) ।

473. Valve.
vaalv. वाल्व ।

474. Front wheel.
saam-né vaa-laa pa-hi-yaa. सामने वाला पहिया ।

475. Rear wheel.
pichh-laa pa-hi-yaa. पिछला पहिया ।

476. Windshield wiper.
vaa-i-par. वाइपर ।

477. Wrench.

rinch. रिंच।

MAIL

478. Where is [the post office] [a mailbox]?

[Daak ghar] [Daak kaa Dib-baa] ka-haan hai?

[डाक घर] [डाक का डिबबा] कहाँ है?

479. To which window should I go?

main kis khiR-kee par jaa-oon?

मैं किस खिड़की पर जाऊँ?

480. I want to send this letter [by surface mail].

main yé chiT-THee [see mél sé] bhéj-naa [chaa-ha-taa (M.)] [chaa-ha-tee (F.)] hoon.

मैं यह चिट्ठी [सी मेल से] भेजना [चाहता] [चाहती] हूँ।

481. —by air mail.

—ha-vaa-ee Daak sé. _ हवाई डाक से।

482. —by special delivery.

—éks-prés Di-li-va-ree sé. _ एक्सप्रेस डिलिवरी से।

483. —by registered mail, reply requested.

—ré-jis-TarD é Dee (acknowledgement due).

रेजिस्टर्ड ए डी।

484. How much postage do I need for [this postcard]?

[is posT-kaarD] par kit-naa Ti-kaT la-gé-gaa?

[इस पोस्टकार्ड] पर कितना टिकट लगेगा?

485. The package contains [printed matter].

is paar-sal mén [ké-val ki-taa-bén] hain.

इस पार्सिल में [केवल किताबें] हैं।

486. —fragile material.
—TooT-nee vaa-lee chee-zén. _ टूटने वाली चीज़ें।

487. I want to insure this for [200 rupees].*
mu-jhé i-sé [do sau rup-yé] kaa bee-maa kar-vaa-naa hai.
मुझे इसे [दो सौ रूपये] का बीमा करवाना है।

488. Give me a receipt.
mu-jhé ra-seed dee-ji-yé.   मुझे रसीद दीजिये।

489. Will it go out [today]?
kyaa yé [aaj] ra-vaa-naa ho-gaa?
क्या यह [आज] रवाना होगा?

490. Give me ten [Rs.2.35] stamps.
mu-jhé [do rup-yé pain-tees pai-sé] ké das Ti-kaT dee-ji-yé.
मुझे [दो रूपये पैन्तीस पैसे] के दस टिकट दीजिये।

491. Where can I get a money order?
ma-nee aar-Dar faarm ka-haan mil-taa hai?
मनी आर्डर फ़ार्म कहाँ मिलता है?

492. Please forward my mail to [Bangalore].
mé-ree Daak [bang-lor] bhéj dee-ji-yé.
मेरी डाक [बँगलोर] भेज दीजिये।

493. The American Express office will hold my mail.
mé-ree Daak a-mé-ri-kan éks-prés kaa daf-tar rok lé-gaa.
मेरी डाक अमेरिकन एक्सप्रेस का दफ़्तर रोक लेगा।

---

* The Indian rupee (Rs.) is divided into 100 paisas. In 1980, the rupee was equivalent to a little over $.12 with about 8 to the U.S. dollar, or about 18 to the British pound and equal to a little over £ .06.

TELEGRAM

494. Where is the telegraph office?
taar ghar ka-haan hai?   तार घर कहाँ है?

495. I would like to send [a telegram].
mu-jhé [taar] bhéj-naa hai.   मुझे [तार] भेजना है।

496. —express telegram.*
—éks-prés taar. _   एक्सप्रेस तार।

497. —a cablegram.
—vi-dé-shee taar. _   विदेशी तार।

498. What is the rate per word?
har shabd ké kit-né pai-sé?   हर शब्द के कितने पैसे?

499. What is the minimum charge?
kam sé kam kit-né pai-sé lag-té hain?
कम से कम कितने पैसे लगते है ॆ?

500. When will a telegram reach [London]?
taar [lan-dan] kab pa-hun-ché-gaa?
तार [लन्दन] कब पहुँचेगा?

TELEPHONE

501. May I use the telephone?
main kyaa Té-lee-fon kar [sak-taa (M.)] [sak-tee (F.)]
hoon?
मैं क्या टेलीफ़ोन कर [सकता] [सकती] हूँ?

---

* A telegram is like a night letter, while an express telegram is
the faster way to send a wire.

502. Will you dial this number for me?

kyaa aap mé-ré li-yé yé nam-bar mi-laa dén-gé?

क्या आप मेरे लिये यह नम्बर मिला देंगे?

503. Operator, get me this number.

aap-ré-Tar mu-jhé yé nam-bar dee-ji-yé.

आपरेटर मुझे यह नम्बर दीजिये।

504. Call me at this number.

mu-jhé is nam-bar par fon kee-ji-yé-gaa.

मुझे इस नम्बर पर फ़ोन कीजियेगा।

505. My telephone number is [24097].

mé-raa nam-bar [do-chaar-shoon-ya-nau-saat] hai.

मेरा नम्बर [दो चार शून्य नौ सात] है।

506. How much is a long-distance call to [Paris]?

[pai-ris] Trank kaal kar-né kaa kyaa daam hai?

[पेरिस] ट्रंक काल करने का क्या दाम है?

507. What is the charge for the first three minutes?

péh-lé teen mi-naT kaa kyaa daam hai?

पहले तीन मिनट का क्या दाम है?

508. They do not answer.

ko-ee u-THaa na-heen ra-haa (OR: ko-ee ja-vaab na-heen dé-taa).

कोई उठा नहीं रहा (कोई जवाब नहीं देता)।

509. The line is busy.

ko-ee baat kar ra-haa hai. कोई बात कर रहा है।

510. Hello (on the telephone).

ha-lo. हलो।

511. You have connected me with the wrong number.

aap né gha-lat nam-bar mi-laa di-yaa.

आप ने ग़लत नम्बर मिला दिया।

512. This is [Mira] speaking. *

ma͞in [mee-raa] bol ra-hee (F.) ho͞on.

मैं [मीरा] बोल रही हूँ।

513. This is [Ajit] speaking. †

ma͞in [a-jeet] bol ra-haa (M.) ho͞on.

मैं [अजीत] बोल रहा हूँ।

514. With whom do you want to speak?

aap kis sé baat ka-ré͞n-gé? आप किस से बात करेंगे?

515. Hold the line.

za-raa fon par THa-hé-ri-yé. ज़रा फ़ोन पर ठहरिये।

516. Dial again.

phir mi-laa-i-yé. फिर मिलाइये।

517. I cannot hear you.

mu-jhé su-naa-ee na-hé͞en dé ra-haa hai.

मुझे सुनाई नहीं दे रहा है।

518. The connection is poor.

laa-in saaf na-hé͞en hai. लाइन साफ़ नहीं है।

519. Speak louder.

zor sé bo-li-yé. ज़ोर से बोलिये।

520. Call him (OR: her) to the phone.

un-hé͞n fon par bu-laa-i-yé. उन्हें फ़ोन पर बुलाइये।

521. He (OR: she) is not here.

vo ya-haa͞n na-hé͞en hai. वह यहाँ नहीं है।

522. There is a telephone call for you.

aap kaa fon aa-yaa hai. आप का फ़ोन आया है।

---

* Common female name.

† Common male name.

523. May I leave a message?

kyaa main san-désh chhoR [sak-taa (M.)] [sak-tee (F.)] hoon?

क्या मैं सन्देश छोड़ [सकता] [सकती] हूँ?

524. Call me back as soon as possible.

jit-nee jal-dee ho sa-ké, mu-jhé fon kee-ji-yé.

जितनी जल्दी हो सके मुझे फ़ोन कीजिये।

525. I will call back later.

main kuchh dér mén fon [ka-roon-gaa (M.)] [ka-roon-gee (F.)].

मैं कुछ देर में फ़ोन [करूँगा] [करूँगी]।

526. I will wait for your call until [four] o'clock.

main [chaar] ba-jé tak aap ké fon kaa in-té-zaar [ka-roon-gaa (M.)] [ka-roon-gee (F.)].

मैं [चार] बजे तक आप के फ़ोन का इन्तेज़ार [करूँगा] [करूँगी]।

HOTEL

527. I am looking for [a good hotel].

main [ach-chhaa ho-Tal] DHoonDH [ra-haa (M.)] [ra-hee (F.)] hoon.

मैं [अच्छा होटल] ढूँढ [रहा] [रही] हूँ।

528. —the best hotel.

—sab sé ach-chhaa ho-Tal. _ सब से अच्छा होटल।

529. —an inexpensive hotel.

—sas-taa ho-Tal. _ सस्ता होटल।

530. —a government guest house (OR: resthouse).

—sar-kaa-ree gésT haa-oos (OR: Daak bang-lo).

सरकारी गेस्ट हाऊस (डाक बैंगलो)।

531. I want to stay in the center of town.

main sha-hér ké beech mén réh-naa [chaa-ha-taa (M.)] [chaa-ha-tee (F.)] hoon.

मैं शहर के बीच में रहना [चाहता] [चाहती] हूँ।

532. I want a quiet location.

mu-jhé shaant ja-gah chaa-hi-yé.

मुझे शान्त जगह चाहिये।

533. I prefer to be close to [the university].

mu-jhé [vish-va-vi-dyaa-lay] ké paas réh-naa pa-sand hai.

मुझे [विश्वविद्यालय] के पास रहना पसन्द है।

534. I have a reservation for tonight.

aaj raat ké li-yé mé-ree ja-gah ra-khee hai.

आज रात के लिये मेरी जगह रखी है।

535. Where is the registration desk?

ri-sép-shan ka-haan hai? रिसेपशन कहाँ है?

536. Fill out this registration form.

yé ré-jis-Tré-shan faarm bha-ri-yé.

यह रेजिस्ट्रेशन फ़ार्म भरिये।

537. Sign here, please.

krip-yaa ya-haan has-taa-kshar kee-ji-yé.

कृपया यहाँ हस्ताक्षर कीजिये।

538. Leave your passport.

ap-naa paas-porT chhoR dee-ji-yé.

अपना पासपोर्ट छोड़ दीजिये।

539. You may pick it up later.

aap baad mén lé lee-ji-yé-gaa.

आप बाद मैं ले लीजियेगा।

540. Do you have [a single room]?

aap ké paas [ék vyak-ti kaa kam-raa] hai?

आप के पास [एक व्यक्ति का कमरा] है?

541. —a double room.

—do vyak-ti-yon̄ kaa kam-raa.

_ दो व्यक्तियों का कमरा।

542. —an air-conditioned room.

—vaa-taa-noo-koo-lit kam-raa. _ वातानुकूलित कमरा।

543. —a suite.

—kam-ron̄ kaa sveeT. _ कमरों का स्वीट।

544. —a quiet room.

—shaant kam-raa. _ शान्त कमरा।

545. —an inside room.

—an-da-roo-nee kam-raa. _ अन्दरूनी कमरा।

546. —an outside room.

—baa-har kaa kam-raa. _ बाहर का कमरा।

547. —a room with a pretty view.

ai-saa kam-raa ja-haan̄ sé sun-dar drish-ya di-khaa-ee dé.

_ ऐसा कमरा जहाँ से सुन्दर दृश्य दिखाई दे।

548. I want a room [with a double bed].

mu-jhé ai-saa kam-raa chaa-hi-yé [jis mén doh-raa pa-lang ho].

मुझे ऐसा कमरा चाहिये जिस मैं [दोहरा पलंग हो]।

549. —with twin beds.

—jis mén do pa-lang hon̄. _ जिस मैं दो पलंग हों।

550. —with a bath.
—jis ké saath *ghu*-sal-*khaa*-naa ho.

जिस के साथ गुसलख़ाना हो ।

551. —with a shower.
—jis mẽn phu-haa-raa-snaan ho.

जिस में फुहारा स्नान हो ।

552. —with running water.
—jis mẽn nal ho.   जिस में नल हो ।

553. —with hot water.
—jis mẽn ga-ram paa-nee kaa nal ho.

जिस में गरम पानी का नल हो ।

554. —with a balcony.
—jis ké saath chhaj-jaa ho.

जिस के साथ छज्जा हो ।

555. —with television.
—jis mẽn Té-lee-vi-zan ho.

जिस में टेलीविज़न हो ।

556. I shall take a room [for one night].
mu-jhé [ké-val ék raat ké li-yé] kam-raa chaa-hi-yé.

मुझे [केवल एक रात के लिये] कमरा चाहिये ।

557. —for several days.
—ka-ee di-nõn ké li-yé.   कई दिनों के लिये ।

558. —for about a week.
—lag-bhag ék haf-té ké li-yé.

लगभग एक हफ़्ते के लिये ।

559. Can I have it [with meals]?
kyaa kam-raa [bho-jan sa-hit] mil sak-taa hai?

क्या कमरा [भोजन सहित] मिल सकता है?

560. —without meals.
—bho-jan ké bi-naa. _ भोजन के बिना।

561. —with breakfast only.
—ké-val su-bah ké naash-té ké saath.
_ केवल सुबह के नारते के साथ।

562. What is the rate [per night]?
[ék raat] kaa kyaa ki-raa-yaa hai?
[एक रात] का क्या किराया है?

563. —per week.
—pra-ti sap-taah (OR: har haf-té).
_ प्रति सप्ताह (हर हफ्ते)।

564. —per month.
—ék ma-hee-né. _ एक महीने।

565. Are tax and service charge included in the bill?
kyaa Taiks aur bakh-shish bhee bil mén joR deen hain?
क्या टैक्स और बख्शिश भी बिल में जोड़ दी हैं?

566. I should like to see the room.
main kam-raa dékh-naa [chaa-ha-taa (M.)] [chaa-ha-tee (F.)] hoon.
मैं कमरा देखना [चाहता] [चाहती] हूं।

567. Have you something [better]?
aap ké paas [is sé béh-tar] kam-raa hai?
आप के पास [इस से बेहतर] कमरा है?

568. —cheaper.
—is sé sas-taa. _ इस से सस्ता।

569. —larger.
—is sé ba-Raa. _ इस से बड़ा।

570. —smaller.
—is sé chho-Taa. _ इस से छोटा ।

571. —on a [higher] [lower] floor.
—[oo-par vaa-lee] [nee-ché vaa-lee] man-zil par.
_ [ऊपर वाली] [नीचे वाली] मन्ज़िल पर ।

572. —with more light.
—is sé aur rosh-nee vaa-laa. इस से और रौशनी वाला ।

573. —more airy.
—is sé zyaa-daa ha-vaa-daar. इस से ज़्यादा हवादार ।

574. —more attractively furnished.
—is sé ach-chhaa sa-jaa hu-aa. इस से अच्छा सजा हुआ ।

575. —with a view of the sea.
—ja-haan sé sa-mu-dra na-zar aa-yé. जहाँ से समुद्र नज़र आये ।

576. It's too noisy.
ya-haan ba-hut shor hai. यहाँ बहुत शोर है ।

577. This is satisfactory.
yé THeek hai. यह ठीक है ।

578. Is there [an elevator]?
kyaa ya-haan [lifT] hai? क्या यहाँ [लिफ़्ट] है?

579. Upstairs.
oo-par. ऊपर ।

580. Downstairs.
nee-ché. नीचे ।

581. What is my room number?

mé-ré kam-ré kaa kyaa nam-bar hai?

मेरे कमरे का क्या नम्बर है?

582. Give me my room key.

kam-ré kee chaa-bee dee-ji-yé. कमरे की चाबी दीजिये।

583. Bring my luggage upstairs.

mé-raa saa-maan oo-par laa-i-yé.

मेरा सामान ऊपर लाइये।

584. Tell the bearer to get my room ready.*

bai-raa sé kéh dee-ji-yé ki mé-raa kam-raa tai-yaar kar dé.

बैरा से कह दीजिये कि मेरा कमरा तैयार कर दे।

585. Wake me [at eight o'clock in the morning].

mu-jhé [aaTH ba-jé su-bah] u-THaa dee-ji-yé-gaa.

मुझे [आठ बजे सुबह] उठा दीजियेगा।

586. Do not awake me until [then].

[tab] tak mu-jhé na-hee͞n ja-gaa-i-yé-gaa.

[तब] तक मुझे नहीं जगाइयेगा।

587. I want [breakfast] in my room.

[su-bah kaa naash-taa] mu-jhé kam-ré me͞n chaa-hi-yé.

[सुबह का नाश्ता] मुझे कमरे में चाहिये।

588. Please send up room service.

krip-yaa bai-raa ko bhéj dee-ji-yé.

कृपया बैरा को भेज दीजिये।

589. Please bring me [some ice].

mu-jhé [kuchh barf] laa dee-ji-yé.

मुझे [कुछ बर्फ़] ला दीजिये।

* A bearer is an all-purpose servant who performs functions of chambermaid, valet, room service, bellhop, etc.

590. I want to speak to [the manager].

mu-jhé [mai-né-jar saa-hab] sé baat kar-nee hai.

मुझे [मैनेजर साहब] से बात करनी है।

591. Do you have a [letter] [message] [parcel] for me?

mé-ré li-yé [chiT-THee] [san-désh] [paar-sal] hai?

मेरे लिये [चिट्ठी] [सन्देश] [पार्सिल] है?

592. Send [a bearer].

[bai-raa] ko bhé-ji-yé.   [बैरा] को भेजिये।

593. —a waiter.

—vé-Tar.   _   वेटर।

594. —a porter.

—ku-lee.   _   कुली।

595. —a messenger.

—san-désh-vaa-hak.   _   सन्देशवाहक।

596. I am expecting [a friend] [a guest].

main [ap-né dost] [ap-né méh-maan] kaa in-té-zaar mén hoon.

मैं [अपने दोस्त] [अपने मेहमान] का इन्तेज़ार में हूं।

597. Has anyone called?

mé-raa fon to na-heen aa-yaa?   मेरा फ़ोन तो नहीं
आया?

598. Send him up.

un-hén oo-par bhéj dee-ji-yé.   उन्हें ऊपर भेज दीजिये।

599. I shall not eat here for lunch.

main ya-haan do-pa-har kaa khaa-naa na-heen [khaa-oon-gaa (M.)] [khaa-oon-gee (F.)].

मैं यहाँ दोपहर का खाना नहीं [खाऊंगा] [खाऊंगी]।

600. May I have [these valuables] put in the hotel safe?

kyaa main [yé qeem-tee chee-zén] ho-Tal kee ti-jo-ree
mén rakh-vaa [sak-taa (M.)] [sak-tee (F.)] hoon?

क्या मै॑ [यह कीमती चीज़ें] होटल की तिजोरी में रखवा
[सकता] [सकती] हूँ?

601. I would like to have my possessions removed from the safe.

mu-jhé ap-nee chee-zén ti-jo-ree sé ni-kal-vaa-nee hain.

मुझे अपनी चीज़ें तिजोरी से निकलवानी है॑ ।

602. When must I check out?

mu-jhé kam-raa kab khaa-lee kar-naa pa-Ré-gaa?

मुझे कमरा कब ख़ाली करना पड़ेगा?

603. I am leaving at [10 o'clock].

main [das ba-jé] jaa [ra-haa (M.)] [ra-hee (F.)] hoon.

मै॑ [दस बजे] जा [रहा] [रही] हूँ।

604. Make out my bill [as soon as possible].

mé-raa bil [ba-hut jal-dee] ba-naa dee-ji-yé.

मेरा बिल [बहुत जल्दी] बना दीजिये।

605. The doorman.

dar-baan.   दरबान ।

HOTEL STAFF

606. The door doesn't lock.

is dar-vaa-zé kaa taa-laa band na-heen ho-taa.

इस दरवाज़े का ताला बन्द नहीं होता।

607. The [toilet] doesn't work.

[flash] kaam na-heen kar-taa. [फ़्लश] काम नहीं करता।

608. The room is [too cold] [too hot].

kam-raa [ba-hut THan-Daa] [ba-hut ga-ram] hai.

कमरा [बहुत ठन्डा] [बहुत गरम] है।

609. Is this drinking water?

kyaa yé pee-né kaa paa-nee hai?

क्या यह पीने का पानी है?

610. There is no hot water.

ga-ram paa-nee na-heen aa ra-haa hai.

गरम पानी नहीं आ रहा है।

611. Spray for insects, please.

fliT kar dee-ji-yé. फ़्लिट कर दीजिये।

612. Wash and iron [this shirt].

[is ka-meez] ko dho kar i-stree kee-ji-yé.

[इस कमीज़] को धो कर इस्त्री कीजिये।

613. Bring me [another blanket].

[ék aur kam-bal] lé aa-i-yé. [एक और कम्बल] ले आइये।

614. Change the sheets.

chaa-da-rén ba-dal dee-ji-yé. चादरें बदल दीजिये।

615. Make the bed.

bis-tar la-gaa dee-ji-yé. बिसतर लगा दीजिये।

616. A bed sheet.

chaa-dar. चादर।

617. A candle.

mom-bat-tee. मोमबत्ती।

618. Some coathangers.

kuchh koT Taang-né-vaa-lé. कुछ कोट टाँगनेवाले।

619. A glass.

gi-laas. गिलास।

620. A pillow.
ta-ki-yaa. तकिया।

621. A pillowcase.
ghi-laaf. गिलाफ़।

622. An adaptor (for electrical appliances).
bij-lee kaa a-Daip-Tar. बिजली का अडैप्टर।

623. (A cake of) soap.
saa-bun (kee baT-Tee). साबुन (की बट्टी)।

624. Toilet paper.
shauch kaa kaa-*ghaz*. शौच का काग़ज़।

625. A towel.
tau-li-yaa. तौलिया।

626. A wash basin.
chi-lam-chee. चिलमची।

627. A washcloth.
chho-Taa tau-li-yaa. छोटा तौलिया।

RENTING AN APARTMENT

628. I want to rent an apartment [with a bathroom].
mu-jhé [*ghu*-sal-*khaa*-né ké saath] ék flaiT ki-raa-yé par
lé-naa chaa-hi-yé.
मुझे [ग़ुसलख़ाने के साथ] एक फ़्लैट किराये पर लेना चाहिये।

629. —with two bedrooms.
—do so-né ké kam-ron̄ ké saath.
    दो सोने के कमरों के साथ।

630. —with a living room.
—bai-THak ké saath.   बैठक के साथ।

631. —with a dining room.
—bho-jan kam-ré ké saath. _ भोजन कमरे के साथ।

632. —with a kitchen.
—ra-so-ee-ghar ké saath. _ रसोईघर के साथ।

633. Do you furnish [the linens] [the dishes]? *
kyaa aap [chaa-da-rén] [bar-tan] bhee dé-té hain?
क्या आप [चादरें] [बर्तन] भी देते है ?

634. Is it [furnished] [unfurnished]?
kyaa vo [sa-jaa hu-aa] [bi-naa ghar ké saa-maan ké saath]
   hai?
क्या वह [सजा हुआ] [बिना घर के सामान के साथ] है?

635. Do we have to sign a lease?
kyaa ha-mén paT-Té par lé-naa pa-Ré-gaa?
क्या हमें पट्टे पर लेना पड़ेगा?

APARTMENT: USEFUL WORDS

636. Alarm clock.
a-laa-ram gha-Ree. अलारम घड़ी।

637. Ashtray.
raakh-daa-nee. राखदानी।

638. Bathtub.
snaan-Tab. स्नान-टब।

639. Bottle opener.
bo-tal khol-né vaa-laa. बोटल खोलने वाला।

640. Broom.
jhaa-Roo. झाड़ू।

641. Can opener.
Teen khol-né vaa-laa. टीन खोलने वाला।

642. Chair.
kur-see. कुर्सी ।

643. Chest of drawers.
kap-R̄on kaa da-raaz. कपड़ों का दराज़ ।

644. Clock.
gha-Ree. घड़ी ।

645. Closet.
al-maa-ree. अलमारी ।

646. Cook.
ra-so-i-yaa (OR: *khaan-saa-maa*). रसोइया (ख़ानसामा) ।

647. Cork (OR: **Stopper**).
kaag (OR: DaaT). काग (डाट) ।

648. Corkscrew.
kaag-pénch. कागपेंच ।

649. Curtains (OR: **Drapes**).
par-dé. परदे ।

650. Cushion.
gad-dee. गद्दी ।

651. Doorbell.
dar-vaa-zé kee ghan-Tee. दरवाज़े की घन्टी ।

652. Fan.
pan-khaa. पन्खा ।

653. Floor.
farsh. फ़र्श ।

654. Hassock.
moo-RHaa. मूढ़ा ।

655. Lamp.
dee-pak. दीपक।

656. Light bulb.
balb. बल्ब।

657. Linens.
chaa-da-re͞n. चादरें।

658. Mosquito net.
ma-sah-ree (OR: mach-chhar-daa-nee).
मसहरी (मच्छरदानी)।

659. Pail (OR: **Bucket**).
baal-Tee. बालटी।

660. Water jug.
su-raa-hee. सुराही।

661. Water pot.
lo-Taa. लोटा।

662. Carpet.
kaa-leen. कालीन।

663. Rug.
da-ree. दरी।

664. Sink.
chi-lam-chee. चिलमची।

665. Switch (light).
svich. स्विच।

666. Table.
méz. मेज़।

667. Tablecloth.
méz-posh. मेज़पोश।

668. Terrace.
chhaj-jaa. छज्जा ।

669. Tray.
thaa-lee (OR: tash-ta-ree). थाली (तश्तरी) ।

670. Vase.
phool-daan. फूलदान ।

671. Venetian blinds.
jhil-mi-lee. झिलमिली ।

672. Whiskbroom.
chho-Taa jhaa-Roo. छोटा झाड़ू ।

673. Window shade.
khiR-kee kaa par-daa. खिड़की का परदा ।

CAFÉ AND BAR

674. Bartender, please give me [something to drink].
baar-main mu-jhé [kuchh pee-né ko] dee-ji-yé.
बारमैन मुझे [कुछ पीने को] दीजिये ।

675. —an alcoholic beverage.*
—sha-raab. _ शराब ।

676. —a cocktail.
—kaak-Tél. _ काक्टेल ।

677. —mineral water.
—chash-mé kaa paa-nee. _ चश्मे का पानी ।

---

* Most liquors and mixed drinks are referred to by their English names.

678. —whiskey [and soda].
—vis-kee [so-Daa]. _ विस्की [सोडा] ।

679. —a gin [and tonic].
—jin [aur To-nik]. _ जिन [और टोनिक] ।

680. —[sweet] [spiced] yogurt drink.
—[mee-THee] [nam-keen] las-see.
_ [मीठी] [नमकीन] लस्सी ।

681. —lemonade.
—shi-kanj-vee (OR: nim-boo paa-nee).
_ शिकंजवी (निम्बू पानी) ।

682. —a fruit drink.
—shar-bat. _ शर्बत ।

683. —a bottle of [Limca]* [Coca-Cola].
—ék bo-tal [lim-kaa] [ko-kaa-ko-laa].
_ एक बोतल [लिमका] [कोका कोला] ।

684. —a beer.
—bi-yar. _ बियर ।

685. —red wine.
—laal sha-raab. _ लाल शराब ।

686. —white wine.
—sa-féd sha-raab. _ सफ़ेद शराब ।

687. —rosé wine.
—gu-laa-bee sha-raab. _ गुलाबी शराब ।

688. Let's have another.
ék aur ho jaa-yé. एक और हो जायें ।

---

* A lemon-flavored carbonated beverage.

RESTAURANT

689. Please recommend a typical restaurant [for dinner].

aap ko-ee ach-chhaa dé-shee bho-ja-naa-lay [raat ké khaa-né ké li-yé] ba-taa-y én.

आप कोई अच्छा देशी भोजनालय [रात के खाने के लिये] बताऐं ।

690. —for breakfast.

—naash-té ké li-yé. ‗ नाश्ते के लिये ।

691. —for European food.

—vi-laa-ya-tee khaa-né ké li-yé.

‗ विलायती खाने के लिये ।

692. Do you serve [lunch]?

kyaa ya-haān [do-pa-har kaa khaa-naa] mil-taa hai?

क्या यहाँ [दोपहर का खाना] मिलता है?

693. At what time is [supper] served?

[raat kaa khaa-naa] kit-né ba-jé mil-taa hai?

[रात का खाना] कितने बजे मिलता है?

694. There are [three] of us.

ham [teen] log haīn. हम [तीन] लोग हैं ।

695. Are you [the waiter] for my table?

kyaa aap ha-maa-ree méz ké [bai-raa] haīn?

क्या आप हमारे मेज़ के [बैरा] हैं?

696. I prefer a table [by the window].

mu-jhé [khiR-kee ké paas vaa-lee] méz zyaa-daa pa-sand hai.

मुझे [खिड़की के पास वाली] मेज़ ज़्यादा पसन्द है ।

697. —in the corner.
—ko-né vaa-lee. _ कोने वाली।

698. —outdoors.
—baa-har vaa-lee. _ बाहर वाली।

699. —indoors.
—an-dar vaa-lee. _ अन्दर वाली।

700. I'd like to wash my hands.
mu-jhé haath dho-né hain. मुझे हाथ धोने है।

701. We want to dine [à la carte].
ham [ap-nee pa-sand kee chee-zén] khaa-naa chaa-ha-té hain.

हम [अपनी पसन्द की चीज़ें] खाना चाहते है।

702. We shall dine [table d'hôte].
ham [poo-raa thaal] khaa-yén-gé.

हम [पूरा थाल] खायेंगे।

703. We want to eat something [light].
ham [hal-kaa] khaa-naa khaa-yén-gé.

हम [हल्का] खाना खायेंगे।

704. What is the specialty of the house?
ya-haan ké vi-shésh pak-vaan kyaa hai?

यहाँ के विशेष पकवान क्या है?

705. What kind of [fish] do you have?
aap ké ya-haan kis pra-kaar kee [machh-lee] hai?

आप के यहाँ किस प्रकार की [मछली] है?

706. Please serve us the meal as quickly as you can.
jit-nee jal-dee ho sa-ké khaa-naa lé aa-i-yé.

जितनी जल्दी हो सके खाना ले आइये।

707. Call the wine steward.
baar-main ko bu-laa-i-yé.   बारमैन को बुलाइये।

708. Bring me [the menu].
[bho-jan soo-chee] laa-i-yé.   [भोजन सूची] लाइये।

709. —the wine list.
—sharab soo-chee. _ शराब सूची।

710. —water [with] [without] ice.
—barf [ké saath] [ké bi-naa] paa-nee.
  _ बर्फ़ [के साथ] [के बिना] पानी।

711. —a napkin.
—naip-kin. _ नैपकिन।

712. —bread.
—Da-bal ro-Tee. _ डबल रोटी।

713. —butter.
—mak-khan. _ मक्खन।

714. —a cup.
—pyaa-laa. _ प्याला।

715. —a fork.
—kaan-Taa. _ कांटा।

716. —a glass.
—gi-laas. _ गिलास।

717. —a [sharp] knife.
—[téz] chhoo-ree. _ [तेज़] छूरी।

718. —a plate.
—pléT. _ प्लेट।

719. —a large (OR: soup) spoon.
—ba-Raa cham-mach. _ बड़ा चम्मच।

720. —a saucer.
—ék pirch. _ एक पिर्च।

721. —a teaspoon.
—chaay kaa cham-mach. _ चाय का चम्मच।

722. I want something [plain].
mu-jhé [saa-daa] khaa-naa chaa-hi-yé.
मुझे [सादा] खाना चाहिये।

723. Is it [from a can]?
yé kyaa [Teen mén] thaa? यह क्या [टीन में] था?

724. Is it [vegetarian food]?
kyaa yé [shaa-kaa-haa-ree bho-jan] hai?
क्या यह [शाकाहारी भोजन] है?

725. —fatty (OR: greasy).
—char-bee-daar. _ चरबीदार।

726. —fresh.
—taa-zaa. _ ताज़ा।

727. —frozen.
—ja-maa hu-aa. _ जमा हुआ।

728. —lean.
—char-bee ké bi-naa. _ चरबी के बिना।

729. —hot (OR: peppery).
—téz. _ तेज़।

730. —very salty.
—ba-hut nam-keen. _ बहुत नमकीन।

731. —spicy.
—ma-saa-lé-daar. मसालेदार।

732. —[very] sweet.
—[ba-hut] mee-THaa. _ [बहुत] मीठा।

733. How is it prepared?
i-sé kai-sé pa-kaa-yaa jaa-taa hai?
इसे कैसे पकाया जाता है?

734. Is it [baked]?
kyaa yé [tan-doo-ree] hai? क्या यह [तनदूरी] है?

735. —boiled.
—ub-laa hu-aa. _ उबला हुआ।

736. —chopped.
—ka-Taa hu-aa. _ कटा हुआ।

737. —fried.
—ta-laa hu-aa. _ तला हुआ।

738. —grilled.
—bhu-naa hu-aa. _ भुना हुआ।

739. —ground.
—pi-saa hu-aa. पिसा हुआ।

740. —roasted.
—tan-doo-ree (OR: bhu-naa hu-aa).
_ तनदूरी (भुना हुआ)।

741. —sautéed.
—chhaun-kaa hu-aa. _ छौंका हुआ।

742. —on a skewer.
—seekh par. _ सीख पर।

743. This is [stale].
yé [baa-see] hai. यह [बासी] है।

744. —too tough.
—ba-hut sakht. _ बहुत सख़्त ।

745. —too dry.
—ba-hut soo-khaa. _ बहुत सूखा ।

746. This is [undercooked] [burned].
yé [kuchh kach-chaa] [ja-laa hu-aa] hai.
यह [कुछ कच्चा] [जला हुआ] है ।

747. A little bit more.
tho-Raa aur. थोड़ा और ।

748. A little bit less.
tho-Raa kam. थोड़ा कम ।

749. Something else.
kuchh aur. कुछ और ।

750. A small portion.
tho-Raa saa. थोड़ा सा ।

751. I have enough.
bas, ba-hut hai (OR: kaa-fee hai).
बस बहुत है (काफ़ी है) ।

752. This is [not clean] [dirty].
yé [saaf na-heen] [gan-daa] hai.
यह [साफ़ नहीं] [गन्दा] है ।

753. This is too cold.
yé ba-hut THan-Daa hai. यह बहुत ठन्डा है ।

754. I did not order this.
main né yé na-heen mang-vaa-yaa thaa.
मै ने यह नहीं मंगवाया था ।

755. You may take this away.
yé lé jaa-i-yé.   यह ले चलिये।

756. Can I get [another vegetable] instead of this?
is ké bad-lé [ko-ee aur tar-kaa-ree] mil sak-tee hai?
इस के बदले [कोई और तरकारी] मिल सकती है?

757. What flavors do you have?
aap ké paas kaun kaun see hain?
आप के पास कौन कौन सी है˙?

758. The check, please.
krip-yaa bil lé aa-i-yé.   कृपया बिल ले आइये।

759. Pay at the cashier's desk.
pai-sé *kha-zaan*-chee ko dee-ji-yé.
पैसे ख़ज़ांची को दीजिये।

760. Is the tip included?
kyaa is mén ba*kh*-shish joR dee hai?
क्या इस में बख़्शिश जोड़ दी है?

761. There is a mistake in the bill.
is bil mén *ghal*-tee hai.   इस बिल में ग़लती है।

762. What are these charges for?
yé pai-sé kyon jo-Ré?   ये पैसे क्यों जोड़े?

763. Keep the change.
baa-qee pai-sé aap rakh lén.   बाक़ी पैसे आप रख लें।

764. The food and service were excellent.
khaa-naa aur sé-vaa ba-hut ach-chhé thé.
खाना और सेवा बहुत अच्छे थे।

SEASONINGS AND SPICES

765. Anise seed.
saunf.   सौंफ़।

766. Asafoetida.
heeng. हींग ।

767. Basil.
tul-see. तुलसी ।

768. Cardamom.
i-laay-chee. इलायची ।

769. Cinnamon.
daal-chee-nee. दालचीनी ।

770. Cloves.
laung. लौंग ।

771. Coriander.
dha-ni-yaa. धनिया ।

772. Cumin seed.
zee-raa. ज़ीरा ।

773. Fenugreek.
mé-thee. मेथी ।

774. Garlic.
léh-sun. लहसुन ।

775. Ginger.
ad-rak. अदरक ।

776. Mace.
jaa-vi-tree. जावित्री ।

777. Mint.
pu-dee-naa. पुदीना ।

778. Mustard.
raa-ee. राई ।

779. Nutmeg.
jaa-ee-phal. जाईफल।

780. Parsley.
aj-mo-daa. अजमोदा।

781. Green chili pepper.
ha-ree mirch. हरी मिर्च।

782. [Black] [Red] pepper.
[kaa-lee] [laal] mirch. [काली] [लाल] मिर्च।

783. Poppyseeds.
khas-khas. खसखस।

784. Saffron.
ké-sar. केसर।

785. Salt.
na-mak. नमक।

786. Sesame seeds.
til. तिल।

787. Sugar.
chee-nee. चीनी।

788. Tamarind.
im-lee. इमली।

789. Tumeric.
hal-dee. हल्दी।

790. Catsup.
Ta-maa-Tar saas. टमाटर सास।

791. Chutney (sauce).
chaT-nee. चटनी।

792. Condiments (OR: Spices).
ma-saa-lé. मसाले ।

793. Oil.
tél. तेल ।

794. (Spicy) pickles.
a-chaar. अचार ।

795. Vinegar.
sir-kaa. सिरका ।

BEVERAGES AND BREAKFAST FOODS

796. [Black] [Iced] coffee.
[bi-naa doodh vaa-lee] [THan-Dee] kaa-fee.
[बिना दूध वाली] [ठन्डी] काफी ।

797. Tea [with milk].
[doodh ké saath] chaay. [दूध के साथ] चाय ।

798. —with cream.
—kreem ké saath. _ क्रीम के साथ ।

799. —with lemon.
—neem-boo ké saath. _ नीमबू के साथ ।

800. —with an artificial sweetener.
—sai-krin ké saath. _ सैक्रीन के साथ ।

801. —with spices.
—ma-saa-lé-daar. _ मसालेदार ।

802. Hot milk.
ga-ram doodh.   गरम दूध ।

803. Fruit juice.
phal kaa ras.   फल का रस ।

804. [Mango] [Orange] [Tomato] juice.
[aam] [san-ta-ré] [Ta-maa-Tar] kaa ras.
[आम] [संतरे] [टमाटर] का रस ।

805. Pastry.
pés-Tree.   पेस्ट्री ।

806. Rolls.
ban.   बन ।

807. Toast.
TosT.   टोस्ट ।

808. Jam.
mu-rab-baa (OR: jaim).   मुरब्बा (जैम) ।

809. Marmalade.
maar-maa-léD.   मार्मिलेड ।

810. Hot cereal (OR: **Porridge**).
da-li-yaa.   दलिया ।

811. Cold cereal.*
kaurn fléks.   कौर्न फ्लेक्स ।

812. (Indian) Pancakes.
maal-pu-é (OR: mee-THaa pa-raa-THaa).
मालपुए (मीठा पराठा) ।

* Corn flakes are the only commonly available Western breakfast cereal.

813. [Soft-boiled] [Hard-boiled] eggs.
[hal-ké ub-lé] [sakht ub-lé] an-Dé.
[हल्के उबले] [सख़्त उबले] अन्डे।

814. Fried eggs.
fraa-ee an-Dé. फ़ाई अन्डे।

815. Poached eggs.
poch an-Dé. पोच अन्डे।

816. Scrambled eggs.
an-Dé kee bhu-ji-yaa. अन्डे की भुजिया।

817. Omelet.
aam-léT. आमलेट।

818. Vegetable cutlets.
sab-zee ké kaT-léT. सब्ज़ी के कटलेट।

819. Steamed rice ball.
iD-lee. इडली।

820. [Stuffed] Rice pancake.
[ma-saa-laa] do-saa.
[मसाला] दोसा।

SOUPS AND SALAD

821. Meat broth.
maans kaa shor-baa. मांस का शोरबा।

822. Chicken soup.
mur-gee kaa shor-baa. मुर्गी का शोरबा।

823. Tomato soup.
Ta-maa-Tar kaa shor-baa. टमाटर का शोरबा।

824. Vegetable soup.
sab-zee kaa shor-baa.   सब्ज़ी का शोरबा।

825. Green salad.
ha-ree sa-laad.   हरी सलाद।

MEATS

826. Beef.*
gaay kaa gosht.   गाय का गोश्त।

827. Ground lamb (OR: **mutton**).
qee-maa.   क़ीमा।

828. Roast leg of lamb.
raan.   रान।

829. Brains.
bhé-jaa.   भेजा।

830. Chops.
chaup.   चौप।

831. Cutlets.
kaT-léT.   कटलेट।

832. Game.
shi-kaar kaa gosht.   शिकार का गोश्त।

833. Heart.
dil.   दिल।

834. Tripe.
o-jha-Ree.   ओझड़ी।

* Not generally available.

835. Kidneys.
gur-dé. गुर्दे।

836. Liver.
ka-lé-jee. कलेजी।

837. Meatballs.
kof-té. कोफ़्ते।

838. Mutton (OR: **Goat meat**).
bak-ré kaa gosht. बकरे का गोश्त।

839. Pork.
su-ar kaa maans. सुअर का मांस।

840. Venison.
hi-ran kaa gosht. हिरन का गोश्त।

POULTRY

841. Chicken.
mur-gee. मुर्गी।

842. Duck.
bat-tak. बत्तक।

843. Game hen.
jang-lee mur-gee. जंगली मुर्गी।

844. Partridge.
tee-tar. तीतर।

845. Quail.
ba-Tér. बटेर।

846. Turkey.
pé-roo. पेरु।

FISH AND SEAFOOD

847. Pomfret.*
paum-fré. पौमफ्रे ।

848. Clams.
sip-pee. सिप्पी ।

849. Cod.
sné-ha-meen. स्नेहमीन ।

850. Crab.
kék-Raa. केकड़ा ।

851. Crayfish.
chin-gaT. चिंगट ।

852. Rehu (a river fish).
ré-hoo (OR: ro-hoo). रेहू (रोहू) ।

853. Herring.
hil-saa. हिलसा ।

854. Lobster.
jhéen-gaa. झींगा ।

855. Oysters.
shuk-ti. शुक्ति ।

856. Prawns (OR: Shrimps).
jhéen-gaa. झींगा ।

857. Salmon.
saa-man. सामन ।

* Distinctions among varieties of fish are seldom made; in inland cities a tasty filet of river fish is served; in coastal areas seafood is available in good restaurants.

858. Sardine.
saar-Deen. सार्डीन ।

859. Sole.
ku-kur-jee-bhee. कुकुरजीभी ।

VEGETABLES

860. Artichoke.
haa-thee-chak. हाथीचक ।

861. Asparagus.
sha-taa-var. शतावर ।

862. Dried beans.
lo-bi-yaa. लोबिया ।

863. Green beans.
sém. सेम ।

864. Beets.
chu-kan-dar. चुकन्दर ।

865. Bitter melon.
ka-ré-laa. करेला ।

866. Cabbage.
band go-bhee. बन्द गोभी ।

867. Carrots.
gaa-jar. गाजर ।

868. Cauliflower.
phool go-bhee. फूल गोभी ।

869. Celery.
sé-la-ree. सेलरी ।

870. Coriander leaves.
ha-raa dha-ni-yaa. हरा धनिया ।

871. Cucumber.
khee-raa (OR: kak-Ree).
खीरा (ककड़ी) ।

872. Eggplant.
bain-gan. बैंगन ।

873. Lettuce.
sa-laad. सलाद ।

874. Mushrooms.
khu-mee. खुमी ।

875. Black dried mushrooms.
guch-chhee. गुच्छी ।

876. Okra.
bhin-Dee. भिंडी ।

877. Olives.
zai-toon. ज़ैतून ।

878. Onions.
pyaaz. प्याज़ ।

879. Peas.
ma-Tar. मटर ।

880. Green pepper.
sim-laa mirch. सिमला मिर्च ।

881. Potatoes.
aa-loo. आलू ।

882. Pumpkin.
kad-doo. कद्दू ।

883. Radish.
moo-lee. मूली ।

884. Spinach.
paa-lak kaa saag. पालक का साग ।

885. Mustard greens.
sar-son kaa saag. सरसों का साग ।

886. Fenugreek greens.
mé-thee kaa saag. मैथी का साग ।

887. Sweet potatoes.
sha-kar-kand. शकरकन्द ।

888. Tomatoes.
Ta-maa-Tar. टमाटर ।

889. Turnips.
shal-jam. शलजम ।

GRAINS AND CEREALS

890. Barley.
jau. जौ ।

891. Chickpeas.
cha-né. चने ।

892. Corn.
ma-ka-ee. मकई ।

893. Lentils.
daal. दाल ।

894. Black lentils.
kaa-lee u-rad. काली उरद ।

895. Yellow lentils.
dhu-lee u-rad.   धुली उरद ।

896. Millet.
baaj-raa.   बाजरा ।

897. Oats.
ja-ee.   जई ।

898. Rice.
chaa-val.   चावल ।

899. Wheat.
gé-hoon.   गेहूँ ।

900. White flour.
mai-daa.   मैदा ।

901. Whole wheat flour.
aa-Taa.   आटा ।

902. Chickpea flour.
bé-san.   बेसन ।

903. Vermicelli.
sé-va-ee.   सेवई ।

FRUITS AND NUTS

904. Almond.
ba-daam.   बदाम ।

905. Apple.
séb.   सेब ।

906. Apricot.
*kh*oo-baa-nee (OR: zard-aa-loo).
खूबानी (ज़र्दआलू) ।

907. Banana.
ké-laa. केला ।

908. Cashew.
kaa-joo. काजू ।

909. Cocoanut.
naa-ri-yal. नारियल ।

910. Custard apple.
sha-ree-faa. शरीफ़ा ।

911. Dates.
kha-joor. खजूर ।

912. Figs.
an-jeer. अन्जीर ।

913. [A half] grapefruit.
[aa-dhaa] cha-ko-traa. [आधा] चकोतरा ।

914. Grapes.
an-goor. अन्गूर ।

915. Guava.
am-rood. अमरूद ।

916. Lemon.
nim-boo. निम्बू ।

917. Lichee nut.
lee-chee. लीची ।

918. Mango.
aam. आम ।

919. Melon.
*kh*ar-boo-zaa. खरबूज़ा ।

920. Orange.
maal-Taa (OR: mu-sam-mee). मालटा (मुसम्मी) ।

921. Papaya.
pa-pee-taa. पपीता ।

922. Peach.
aa-Roo. आड़ू ।

923. Peanuts.
moong-pha-lee. मूंगफली ।

924. Pear.
naash-paa-tee. नाश्पाती ।

925. Pineapple.
a-naa-naas. अनानास ।

926. Pistachio nuts.
pis-taa. पिस्ता ।

927. Plum.
aa-loo bu-*khaa*-raa. आलू बुझारा ।

928. Pomegranate.
a-naar. अनार ।

929. Raisins.
kish-mish. किश्मिश ।

930. Sugarcane.
gan-naa. गन्ना ।

931. Strawberries.
sTraa-bé-ree. स्ट्राबेरी ।

932. Tangerine.
san-ta-raa. संतरा।

933. Walnuts.
akh-roT. अखरोट।

934. Watermelon.
tar-booz. तरबूज़।

DESSERTS

935. Cake.
kék. केक।

936. Caramel custard.
kai-raa-mal kas-TarD. कैरामल कस्टर्ड।

937. Cupcakes (OR: **Petit fours**).
pés-Tree. पेस्ट्री।

938. Cookies.
bis-kuT. बिस्कुट।

939. Ice cream.
aa-is-kreem. आइसक्रीम।

940. Pudding.
pu-Ding. पुडिंग।

941. Sweets (OR: **Dessert**).
mi-THaa-ee. मिठाई।

INDIAN FOODS*

APPETIZERS AND SNACKS

942. aa-loo chaaT. आलू चाट।
Fried peas-and-mashed-potato snack.

943. bain-gan bhar-taa. बैंगन भरता।
Mashed, curried eggplant.

944. gol-gap-pé. गोलगप्पे।
Small, fried pastry puffs soaked in tamarind-flavored water.

945. [qee-maa] [ma-Tar aa-loo] sa-mo-saa.
[क़ीमा] [मटर आलू] समोसा।
[Chopped-meat] [peas-and-potato] stuffed fried pastry.

946. paa-paR. पापड़।
Thin, crisp wafer made of lentil flour.

947. [pa-neer] [sab-zee kaa] pa-ko-Raa.
[पनीर][सब्ज़ी की] पकोड़ा।
[Cheese-filled] [vegetable] fritter.

948. pu-dee-naa dha-ni-yaa kee chaT-nee.
पुदीना धनिया की चटनी।
Fresh mint and coriander sauce used on snacks.

949. rai-taa (OR: **da-hee**). रैता (दही)।
Spiced yogurt and vegetable salad (OR: plain yogurt).

* The following sections (pp. 90–94) form a list containing names and descriptions of some typical North Indian food specialties. While it does not claim to be comprehensive, it is hoped it will encourage the users of this book to sample the varied and outstanding cuisines of India. To facilitate use, the Hindi name is given first, then the English description.

MEAT ENTREES

950. bhin-Dee gosht. भिंडी गोश्त।
Okra and meat curry.

951. bo-Tee ka-baab. बोटी कबाब.
Shish kabab.

952. qee-maa ma-Tar. क़ीमा मटर।
Peas and chopped-meat curry.

953. nar-gi-see kofta. नरगिसी कोफ़ता।
Hard-boiled eggs coated in chopped meat and curried.

954. ro-gan josh. रोगन जोश।
Mutton curry.

955. seekh ka-baab. सीख़ कबाब।
Spiced chopped meat shaped around a long, square
    skewer and grilled.

956. shaa-hee kor-maa. शाही कोरमा।
Mutton curried in thick yogurt gravy.

957. shaa-mee ka-baab. शामी कबाब।
Fried chopped-meat and lentil patty.

POULTRY ENTREES

958. mak-kha-nee mur-gaa. मक्खनी मुर्गा।
Chicken in butter and tomato sauce.

959. murg mu-sal-lam. मुर्ग मुसल्लम।
Whole roast chicken.

960. mur-gee do pyaa-zaa. मुर्गी दो प्याज़ा ।
Chicken and onion curry.

961. tan-doo-ree mur-gaa. तन्दूरी मुर्गा ।
Marinated, grilled chicken.

FISH ENTREES

962. mach-chhee tik-kaa. मच्छी तिक्का ।
Marinated, roasted chunks of fish.

963. ma-saa-lé-daar jheen-gaa. मसालेदार झींगा ।
Curried prawns.

VEGETABLE ENTREES

964. a-loo go-bhee. आलू गोभी ।
Potato and cauliflower curry.

965. bhu-ji-yaa. भुजिया ।
Dry vegetable curry.

966. daal. दाल ।
Curried lentils.

967. kaab-lee cha-naa. काबुली चना ।
Curried chickpeas.

968. ma-Tar pa-neer. मटर पनीर ।
Peas and cheese curry.

969. sab-zee tik-kee. सब्ज़ी तिक्की ।
Vegetable cutlet.

970. tar-kaa-ree. तरकारी ।
Mixed vegetable curry.

RICE ENTREES AND BREADS

971. bir-yaa-nee. बिरमानी ।
Rich mutton pilaf.

972. kash-mi-ree pu-laa-o. कश्मिरी पुलाव ।
Pilaf of nuts, dried fruit and mutton.

973. khi-cha-Ree. खिचड़ी ।
Rice and lentil porridge.

974. mach-chhee ma-Tar pu-laa-o. मच्छी मटर पुलाव ।
Seafood and peas pilaf.

975. pu-laa-o. पुलाव ।
Plain rice pilaf.

976. yakh-nee pu-laa-o. यख्नी पुलाव ।
Mutton pilaf simmered in stock.

977. cha-paa-tee (OR: **phul-kaa**). चपाती (फुलका) ।
Flat, wholewheat baked bread.

978. naan. नान ।
Oven-baked, yeast bread.

979. pa-raa-THaa. परांठा ।
Flat, fried wholewheat bread.

980. poo-Ree. पूड़ी ।
Deep-fried, puffed wholewheat bread.

981. tan-doo-ree ro-Tee. तन्दूरी रोटी ।
Oven-baked wholewheat bread.

DESSERTS AND SWEETS

982. bar-fee [ba-daam] [pis-taa].

बर्फी [बदाम] [पिस्ता] ।

[Almond] [pistachio] candy.

983. fir-nee. फ़िरनी ।

Smooth farina pudding.

984. gaa-jar kaa hal-vaa. गाजर का हलवा ।

Sweet carrot pudding.

985. gu-laab jaa-mun. गुलाब जामुन ।

Deep-fried dough balls in rosewater syrup.

986. kul-fee. कुल्फ़ी ।

Ice cream made of milk, almonds and pistachios, garnished with vermicelli and rosewater syrup.

987. kheer. खीर ।

Rice pudding.

988. ja-lé-bee. जलेबी ।

Deep-fried dough swirls in rosewater syrup.

989. ras-gul-laa. रसगुल्ला ।

Cottage cheese balls in sweet syrup.

SIGHTSEEING

990. I want a licensed guide [who knows English].
mu-jhé ék pra-maa-Nit gaa-iD chaa-hi-yé [jo an-gré-zee jaan-taa ho].

मुझे एक प्रमाणित गाइड चाहिये [जो अँग्रेज़ी जानता हो] ।

991. How long will the excursion take?
sa-far men kit-naa sa-may la-gé-gaa?
सफ़र में कितना समय लगेगा?

992. Do I have to book in advance?
kyaa mu-jhé péh-lé sé ja-gah lé-nee pa-Ré-gee?
क्या मुझे पहले से जगह लेनी पड़ेगी?

993. Are admission tickets and a snack included?
kyaa is men pra-vésh Ti-kaT aur naash-taa bhee shaa-mil hain?
क्या इस में प्रवेश टिकट और नाश्ता भी शामिल है?

994. What is the charge for a trip [to the Taj Mahal]?
[taaj ma-hél kee] sair kar-né kaa kyaa ki-raa-yaa hai?
[ताज महल की] सैर करने का क्या किराया है?

995. —to the mountain.
—pa-haaR kee. _   पहाड़ की ।

996. —to the sea.
—sa-mu-dra kee. _   समुद्र की ।

997. —around the city.
—sha-hér ké ird-gird. _   शहर के इर्दगिर्द ।

998. Pick me up [tomorrow] at my hotel at 8 A.M.
[kal] su-bah aaTH ba-jé ho-Tal sé mu-jhé lé-né aa-naa.
[कल] सुबह आठ बजे होटल से मुझे लेने आना ।

999. Show me the sights of interest.
mu-jhé ya-haan ké dar-sha-nee-ya sthaan di-khaa-i-yé.
मुझे यहाँ के दर्शनीय स्थान दिखाइये ।

1000. What is that building?
vo kaun-see i-maa-rat hai?
वह कौनसी इमारत है?

1001. How old is it?

kit-nee praa-cheen hai? कितनी प्राचीन है?

1002. Can we go in?

kyaa ham an-dar jaa sak-té hain?

क्या हम अन्दर जा सकते है ?

1003. I am interested in [architecture].

mu-jhé [vaas-tu-ka-laa] mén dil-chas-pee hai.

मुझे [वास्तुकला] में दिलचस्पी है ।

1004. —archeology.

—pu-raa-tat-va. _ पुरतत्त्व ।

1005. —sculpture.

—shilp-ka-laa. _ शिल्पकला ।

1006. —painting.

—chi-tra-ka-laa. _ चित्रकला ।

1007. —folk art.

—lok ka-laa. _ लोक कला ।

1008. —native arts and handicrafts.

—dé-shee ka-laa aur dast-kaa-ree.

_ देशी कला और दस्तकारी ।

1009. —modern art.

—aa-dhu-nik ka-laa. _ अधुनिक कला ।

1010. I should like to see [the park].

main [baa-gee-chaa] dékh-naa [chaa-ha-taa (M.)] [chaa-ha-tee (F.)] hoon.

मै [बागीचा] देखना [चाहता] [चाहती] हूं ।

1011. —the island.

—Taa-poo. _ टापू ।

1012. —the caves.
—gu-hé. _ गुहे ।

1013. —the statue.
—moor-ti. _ मूर्ति ।

1014. —the library.
—pus-ta-kaa-lay (OR: laa-i-bré-ree).
_ पुस्तकालय (लाइब्रेरी) ।

1015. —the ruins.
—khanD-har. _ खंडहर ।

1016. —the castle (OR: **fort**).
—ki-laa. _ किला ।

1017. —the palace.
—ma-hél. _ महल ।

1018. —the zoo.
—chi-Ri-yaa-ghar. _ चिड़ियाघर ।

1019. Let's take a walk around [the botanical garden].
cha-li-yé [baa-gee-ché] kee sair ka-rén.
चलिये [बागीचे] की सैर करें ।

1020. Is it a tourist trap?
yé kyaa vi-dé-shi-yon̄ ko pha-saa-né ké li-yé hai?
यह क्या विदेशियों को फ़साने के लिये है?

1021. A beautiful view!
kit-naa sun-dar drish-ya! कितना सुन्दर दृश्य ।

1022. Very beautiful!
ba-hut sun-dar! बहुत सुन्दर ।

1023. Very interesting!
ba-hut ma-no-ran-jak! बहुत मनोरंजक ।

1024. Magnificent!

ba-hut shaan-daar! बहुत शानदार।

1025. We are enjoying ourselves.

ha-mén ba-hut aa-nand aa ra-haa hai.

हमें बहुत आनन्द आ रहा है।

1026. I am bored.

mé-raa jee oob ga-yaa hai. मेरा जी उब गया है।

1027. When does the museum [open] [close]?

san-gra-haa-lay kab [khul-taa] [band ho-taa] hai?

संग्रहालय कब [खुलता] [बन्द होता] है?

1028. Is this the way [to go in] [to go out]?

yé kyaa [bhee-tar jaa-né] [baa-har jaa-né] kaa raas-taa hai?

यह क्या [भीतर जाने] [बाहर जाने] का रास्ता है?

1029. Let's visit the fine arts gallery.

cha-li-yé la-lit-ka-laa san-gra-haa-lay cha-lén.

चलिये ललितकला संग्रहालय चलें।

1030. Let's stay longer.

kuchh dér aur THa-hé-rén. कुछ देर और ठहरें।

1031. Let's leave now.

a-bhee cha-lén. अभी चलें।

1032. We must return by 5 o'clock.

ha-mén paanch ba-jé tak za-roor lauT-naa hai.

हमें पाँच बजे तक ज़रूर लौटना है।

1033. If there is time, let's rest a while.

a-gar sa-may hai to kuchh dér tak aa-raam kar lén.

अगर समय है तो कुछ देर तक आराम कर लें।

WORSHIP

1034. Altar.
vé-dee. वेदी ।

1035. Church.
gir-jaa. गिर्जा ।

1036. Choral music.
sam-vét bha-jan. समवेत भजन ।

1037. Hindu religious hymns.
bha-jan (OR: kir-tan). भजन (किरतन) ।

1038. Muslim religious song.
kav-vaa-lee. कव्वाली ।

1039. Communion.
pra-bhu-bhoj. प्रभुभोज ।

1040. Confession.
paap-svee-kaar. पापस्वीकार ।

1041. Mass.
mis-saa. मिस्सा ।

1042. Prayers.
praarth-naa-én. प्रार्थनाएं ।

1043. Prayer book.
praarth-naa-pus-tak. प्रार्थना-पुस्तक ।

1044. Priest.
paa-dree. पादरी ।

1045. Hindu priest.
pu-ro-hit. पुरोहित ।

1046. Muslim priest.
i-maam (OR: maul-vee). इमाम (मौलवी)।

1047. Rabbi.
rab-bee. रब्बी।

1048. Religious school (for Hindus).
aash-ram (OR: maTH). आश्रम (मठ)।

1049. Religious school (for Muslims).
mad-raa-saa. मदरासा।

1050. Religious school (for girls).
kaan-vénT-skul. कानवेन्ट-स्कूल।

1051. Sermon.
prav-chan. प्रवचन।

1052. Services.
poo-jaa. पूजा।

1053. Hindu temple.
man-dir. मन्दिर।

1054. Mosque.
mas-jid. मस्जिद।

1055. Sikh temple.
gur-dvaa-raa. गुरद्वारा।

1056. A Christian.
ee-saa-ee. ईसाई।

1057. A Hindu.
hin-doo. हिन्दू।

1058. A Moslem.
mu-sal-maan. मुसलमान।

1059. A Jew.
ya-hu-dee. यहुदी।

1060. A holy man.
saa-dhoo. साधू।

ENTERTAINMENTS

1061. Is there [a matinée] today?
aaj kyaa [do-pa-har kaa khél] ho-gaa?
आज क्या [दोपहर का खेल] होगा?

1062. Has [the show] begun?
kyaa [khél] shu-roo ho ga-yaa hai?
क्या [खेल] शुरु हो गया है?

1063. What is playing now?
is sa-may kyaa chal ra-haa hai?
इस समय क्या चल रहा है?

1064. Have you any seats for [tonight]?
[aaj raat] ké li-yé ja-gah hai?
[आज रात] के लिये जगह है?

1065. What is the price of [a balcony seat]?*
[bail-ka-nee ké Ti-kaT] kaa kyaa daam hai?
[बैल्कनी के टिकट] का क्या दाम है?

1066. —an orchestra seat.
—nee-ché kee seeT. _ नीचे की सीट।

---

* In Indian cinema houses the balcony is considered the best
viewing area, and those closest to the screen are least desirable.

1067. —a box.
—bauks seeT. _ बौक्स सीट।

1068. Not too far from the stage.
manch sé zyaa-daa door na-heen.
मंच से ज़्यादा दूर नहीं।

1069. Here is my stub.
mé-raa Ti-kaT yé hai. मेरा टिकट यह है।

1070. Can I see and hear well from there?
kyaa main va-haan sé ach-chhee ta-rah dékh-sun [sa-koon-gaa (M.)] [sa-koon-gee (F.)]?
क्या मैं वहाँ से अच्छी तरह देख-सुन [सकूँगा] [सकूँगी]?

1071. Follow [the usher].
[pra-vé-shak] ké saath jaa-i-yé. [प्रवेशक] के साथ जाइये।

1072. Is smoking permitted here?
kyaa ya-haan dhu-mar-paan kar sak-té hain?
क्या यहाँ धुम्रपान कर सकते हैं?

1073. How long is the intermission?
in-Tar-val kit-naa lam-baa hai?
इन्टरवल कितना लम्बा है?

1074. When does the program [begin] [end]?
kaar-ya-kram kab [aa-rambh] [sa-maapt] ho-gaa?
कार्यक्रम कब [आरंभ] [समाप्त] होगा?

1075. Everyone enjoyed the show.
khél sab lo-gon ko pa-sand aa-yaa.
खेल सब लोगों को पसन्द आया।

1076. The box office.
Ti-kaT-ghar. टिकटघर।

1077. The circus.
sar-kas. सरकस ।

1078. The concert.
san-geet kaar-ya-kram. संगीत कार्यक्रम ।

1079. The classical (Indian) dance.*
nrit-ya. नृत्य ।

1080. The folk dances.
lok nrit-ya. लोक नृत्य ।

1081. Vocal music.
kanTH-san-geet. कंठसंगीत ।

1082. The [beginning] [end] of the line.
pank-ti kaa [shu-roo] [aa-*khir*].
पंक्ति का [शुरू] [आख़िर] ।

1083. The movies.
si-né-maa (OR: fi-lam). सिनेमा (फ़िल्म) ।

1084. The nightclub.
naa-iT klab. नाइट क्लब ।

1085. Music hall.
san-geet bha-van. संगीत भवन ।

1086. The performance.
pra-dar-shan (OR: khél). प्रदर्शन (खेल) ।

1087. The private club.
jim-*khaa*-naa. जिम्ख़ानT ।

---

* Classical Indian dance has distinct regional styles. Some major ones are: *bhaa-rat naaT-yam*, southern devotional style, *ka-thak*, northern courtly style and *ka-tha-ka-lee*, epic dance-drama.

1088. The puppet show.
kaTH-put-lee kaa naach.   कठपुतली का नाच ।

1089. The reserved seat.
aa-ra-kshit ja-gah.   आरक्षित जगह ।

1090. The sports event.
khél (OR: maich).   खेल (मैच) ।

1091. Standing room.
kha-Ré ho-né kee ja-gah.   खड़े होने की जगह ।

1092. The theater.
naaT-ya ghar.   नाट्य घर ।

1093. The variety show.
vi-vidh ma-no-ran-jan.   विविध मनोरंजन ।

SPORTS AND GAMES

1094. We want to play [soccer].
ham [fuT-baal] khél-naa chaa-ha-té hain.

हम [फ़ुटबाल] खेलना चाहते हैं ।

1095. —basketball.
—baa-skiT-baal.   _ बास्किटबाल ।

1096. —cards.
—taash.   _ ताश ।

1097. —golf.
—gaalf.   _ गाल्फ़ ।

1098. —ping-pong.
—Té-bal Té-nis.   _ टेबल टेनिस ।

1099. —tennis.
—Té-nis. _ टेनिस ।

1100. —cricket.
—kri-kéT. _ क्रिकेट ।

1101. Do you play [chess]?
kyaa aap [shat-ranj] khél-té hain?
क्या आप [शतरंज] खेलते है'?

1102. —carom.*
—kai-ram. _ कैरम ।

1103. —bridge.
—brij. _ ब्रिज ।

1104. Let's go swimming.
cha-li-yé tair-né cha-lén. चलिये तैरने चलें ।

1105. Let's go to [the swimming pool].
cha-li-yé [pool mén tair-né] cha-lén.
चलिये [पूल में तैरने] चलें ।

1106. —the beach.
—sa-mu-dra ké ki-naa-ré. _ समुद्र के किनारे ।

1107. —the horse races.
—gho-Ron kee dauR. _ घोड़ों की दौड़ ।

1108. —the soccer game.
—fuT-baal maich. _ फुटबाल मैच ।

* A popular Indian game similar to billiards but played with checkers.

1109. I need [golf equipment].
mu-jhé [gaalf khél-né kaa saa-maan] chaa-hi-yé.

मुझे [गाल्फ़ खेलने का सामान] चाहिये।

1110. —fishing tackle.
—machh-lee pa-kaR-né kaa saa-maan.

_ मछली पकड़ने का सामान।

1111. —a tennis racket.
—Té-nis kaa bal-laa.   टेनिस का बल्ला।

1112. Can we go [fishing]?
kyaa ham [machh-lee kaa shi-kaar] kar sak-té hain?

क्या हम [मछली का शिकार] कर सकते हैं?

1113. —horseback riding.
—ghuR sa-vaa-ree.   घुड़ सवारी।

1114. —roller skating.
—pa-hi-yé kee ské-Ting.   पहिये की स्केटिंग।

1115. —ice skating.
—barf par ské-Ting.   बर्फ़ पर स्केटिंग।

1116. —sledding.
—sléD gaa-Ree.   स्लेड गाड़ी।

1117. —skiing.
—barf kee pa-Tree.   बर्फ़ की पट्री।

HIKING AND CAMPING

1118. How far a walk is it to the [youth hostel]?
ya-haan sé [yooth hos-Tél] pai-dal kit-nee door hai?

यहाँ से [यूथ होस्टेल] पैदल कितनी दूर है?

1119. Are sanitary facilities available?
shau-chaa-lay kaa pra-bandh hai?
शौचालय का प्रबन्ध है?

1120. Campsite.
shi-vir sthaan (OR: Dé-raa). शिविर स्थान (डेरा) ।

1121. Camping equipment.
shi-vir kaa saa-maan. शिविर का सामान ।

1122. Camping permit.
shi-vir kar-né kaa par-miT. शिविर करने का परमिट ।

1123. Cooking utensils.
bar-tan. बरतन ।

1124. Firewood.
lak-Ree. लकड़ी ।

1125. Footpath.
pag-Dan-Dee. पगडंडी ।

1126. Hike.
pad-yaa-traa (OR: pai-dal sair). पदयात्रा (पैदल सैर) ।

1127. Matches.
maa-chis kee tee-lee. माचिस की तीली ।

1128. Picnic.
pik-nik (OR: van-bho-jan). पिकनिक (वनभोजन) ।

1129. Rubbish.
koo-Raa. कूड़ा ।

1130. Rubbish receptacle.
koo-Ré-daan. कूड़ेदान ।

1131. Shortcut.
chho-Taa raas-taa. छोटा रास्ता ।

1132. Tent.
tam-boo. तम्बू ।

1133. Thermos.
thar-mas. थर्मस ।

1134. Drinking water.
pee-né kaa paa-nee. पीने का पानी ।

1135. Forest.
jan-gal. जंगल ।

1136. Lake.
jheel (OR: taa-laab). झील (तालाब) ।

1137. Mountain.
pa-haaR. पहाड़ ।

1138. River.
na-dee. नदी ।

1139. Stream.
chash-maa (OR: chho-Tee na-dee).
चश्मा (छोटी नदी) ।

BANK AND MONEY

1140. Where can I change foreign money?
vi-dé-shee pai-sé main ka-haan ba-dal [sak-taa (M.)] [sak-tee (F.)] hoon?
विदेशी पैसे में कहाँ बदल [सकता] [सकती] हूँ?

1141. What is the exchange rate on [the dollar] [the pound]?

[Daa-lar] [paunD] ba-dal-né kaa kyaa bhaa-o hai?

[डालर] [पौंड] बदलने का क्या भाव है?

1142. Will you cash [a personal check] [a travellers' check]?

aap [mé-raa chék] [sai-laa-ni-yon kaa chék] lén-gé?

आप [मेरा चेक] [सैलानियों का चेक] लोगे?

1143. I have [a bank draft] [a letter of credit].

mé-ré paas [baink DraafT] [saakh-pa-tra] hai.

मेरे पास [बैन्क ड्राफ्ट] [साखपत्र] है।

1144. I would like to exchange [twenty] dollars.

main [bees] Daa-lar ba-dal-vaa-naa [chaa-ha-taa (M.)] [chaa-ha-tee (F.)] hoon.

मैं [बीस] डालर बदलवाना [चाहता] [चाहती] हूं।

1145. Please give me [large bills].

mu-jhé [ba-Ré noT] dee-ji-yé. मुझे [बड़े नोट] दीजिये।

1146. —small bills.

—chho-Té noT. _ छोटे नोट।

1147. —small change.

—khu-lé pai-sé (OR: réz-gaa-ree). _ खुले पैसे (रेज़गारी)।

SHOPPING

1148. Show me the [hat] displayed in the front of the store.

vo [To-pee] di-khaa-i-yé jo du-kaan ké saam-né la-gee hai.

वह [टोपी] दिखाइये जो दुकान के सामने लगी है।

1149. Can you [help me]?

kyaa aap [mé-ree sa-haa-ya-taa kar] sak-té hain?

क्या आप [मेरी सहायता कर] सकते हैं?

1150. I am just looking around.

main sirf dékh [ra-haa (M.)] [ra-hee (F.)] hoon.

मैं सिर्फ़ देख [रहा] [रही] हूँ।

1151. I shall come back later.

main phir lauT kar [aa-oon-gaa (M.)] [aa-oon-gee (F.)].

मैं फिर लौट कर [आऊँगा] [आऊँगी]।

1152. I've been waiting [a long time].

main [ba-hut dér sé] in-té-zaar kar [ra-haa (M.)] [ra-hee (F.)] hoon.

मैं [बहुत देर से] इन्तेज़ार कर [रहा] [रही] हूँ।

1153. What brand do you have?

aap ké paas kaun-see chhaap hai?

आप के पास कौनसी छाप है?

1154. How much is [it]?

[is] kaa kyaa daam hai? [इस] का क्या दाम है?

1155. What is the price [per piece]?

[prat-yék (OR: har ék)] kaa kyaa daam hai?

[प्रत्येक (हर एक)] का क्या भाव है?

1156. —per meter.

—ék mee-Tar. _ एक मीटर।

1157. —per pound.

—aa-dhé ki-lo. _ आधे किलो।

1158. —per kilo.

—ék ki-lo (OR: sér). एक किलो (सेर)।

1159. —per package.

—ék Dib-bi-yé. एक डिब्बिये।

1160. —per bunch.
—ék guch-chhé. _ एक गुच्छे।

1161. How much do I have to pay [altogether]?
[sab mi-laa-kar] kit-né pai-sé dé-né hain?
[सब मिलाकर] कितने पैसे देने है॰?

1162. It is [too expensive] [cheap] [reasonable].
yé [ba-hut ma-hén-gaa] [sas-taa] [THeek] hai.
यह [बहुत महंगा] [सस्ता] [ठीक] है।

1163. Is that your lowest price?
yé kam sé kam daam hai? मह कम से कम दाम है?

1164. Will you give a discount?
aap kuchh chhooT dén-gé? आप कुछ छूट दैंगे?

1165. I [do not] like that.
mu-jhé vo pa-sand [na-heen] hai.
मुझे वह पसन्द [नहीं] है।

1166. Have you something [better]?
is sé ko-ee [ba-RHi-yaa] hai? इस से कोई [बढ़िया] है?

1167. —cheaper.
—sas-taa. _ सस्ता।

1168. —more fashionable.
—zyaa-daa fai-shan-vaa-laa. _ ज़्यादा फैशनवाला।

1169. —softer.
—mu-laa-yam. _ मुलायम।

1170. —stronger.
—maz-boot. _ मज़बूत।

1171. —heavier.
—bhaa-ree. _ भारी।

1172. —lighter (in weight).
—hal-kaa. _ हल्का ।

1173. —tighter.
—chust (OR: tang). _ चुस्त (तंग) ।

1174. —looser.
—DHee-laa. _ ढीला ।

1175. —lighter in color.
—hal-ké rang kaa. _ हल्के रंग का ।

1176. —darker.
—géh-ré rang kaa. _ गहरे रंग का ।

1177. Do you have this in [my size]?
kyaa aap ké paas [mé-ré naap] kaa hai?
क्या आप के पास [मेरे नाप] का है?

1178. —women's sizes.
—aur-ton̄ ké naap. _ औरतों के नाप ।

1179. —a larger size.
—is sé ba-Ré naap. _ इस से बड़े नाप ।

1180. —a smaller size.
—is sé chho-Té naap. _ इस से छोटे नाप ।

1181. Can you order it in [another color]?
kyaa aap [ki-see aur rang mén] mang-vaa sak-té hain?
क्या आप [किसी और रंग में] मंगवा सकते है ?

1182. —a different style.
—doos-ré DHang kaa. _ दूसरे ढंग का ।

1183. Where is the fitting room?
Traa-ee kar-né kaa kam-raa ka-haan̄ hai?
ट्राई करने का कमरा कहां है?

1184. May I try it on?

kyaa main pa-hén kar dékh [sak-taa (M.)] [sak-tee (F.)] hoon?

क्या मैं पहन कर देख [सकता] [सकती] हूँ?

1185. It does not fit (for ready-made garments).

yé naap mé-ré li-yé THeek na-heen.

यह नाप मेरे लिये ठीक नहीं।

1186. It does not fit (for tailor-made garments).

yé THeek ta-rah sé poo-raa na-heen aa-taa.

यह ठीक तरह से पूरा नहीं आता।

1187. It is [too short].

yé [kam lam-baa] hai. यह [कम लम्बा] है।

1188. —too long.

—ba-hut lam-baa. _ बहुत लम्बा।

1189. —too big.

—ba-hut ba-Raa. _ बहुत बड़ा।

1190. —too small.

—ba-hut chho-Taa. _ बहुत छोटा।

1191. Please take the measurements.

krip-yaa naap lee-ji-yé. कृपया नाप लीजिये।

1192. The length.

lam-baan (OR: lam-baa-ee). लम्बान (लम्बाई)।

1193. The width.

chau-Raan (OR: chau-Raa-ee). चौड़ान (चौड़ाई)।

1194. Will it shrink?

kyaa yé si-ku-Ré-gaa? क्या यह सिकुड़ेगा?

1195. Will it break?
kyaa yé TooT jaa-yé-gaa? क्या यह टूट जायेगा?

1196. Is it [new]?
kyaa yé [na-yaa] hai? क्या यह [नया] है?

1197. —handmade.
—haath kaa ba-naa. _ हाथ का बना।

1198. —antique.
—praa-cheen. _ प्राचीन।

1199. —a replica.
—pra-ti-kri-ti. _ प्रतिकृति।

1200. —an imitation.
—naq-lee. _ नकली।

1201. Is this colorfast?
kyaa is kaa rang pak-kaa hai?
क्या इस का रंग पक्का है?

1202. I like it.
mu-jhé pa-sand hai. मुझे पसन्द है।

1203. Please have this ready soon.
i-sé jal-dee tai-yaar kar-vaa dee-ji-yé.
इसे जल्दी तैयार करवा दीजिये।

1204. How much time will it take to fix it?
i-sé THeek kar-né men kit-naa sa-may la-gé-gaa?
इसे ठीक करने में कितना समय लगेगा?

1205. Does the price include alterations?
kyaa THeek kar-né kaa daam qee-mat men shaa-mil hai?
क्या ठीक करने का दाम कीमत में शामिल है?

1206. I cannot decide.

main nish-chay na-heen kar paa [ra-haa (M.)] [ra-hee (F.)] hoon.

मैं निश्चय नहीं कर पा [रहा] [रही] हूँ।

1207. I'll wait until it is ready.

main tai-yaar ho-né tak [THa-hé-roon-gaa (M.)] [THa-hé-roon-gee (F.)].

मैं तैयार होने तक [ठहरूँगा] [ठहरूँगी]।

1208. Wrap this.

i-sé baandh dén. इसे बांध दें।

1209. Where do I pay?

main pai-sé ka-haan a-daa ka-roon? मैं पैसे कहाँ अदा करूँ?

1210. Do I pay [the salesman]?

kyaa main [béch-né-vaa-lé] ko pai-sé doon? क्या मैं [बेचनेवाले] को पैसे दूँ?

1211. —saleswoman.

—béch-né-vaa-lee. — बेचनेवाली।

1212. —the shopkeeper (OR: proprietor).

—du-kaan-daar. — दुकानदार।

1213. Will you take a [credit card]?

kyaa aap [kré-DiT kaarD] lé-té hain? क्या आप [क्रेडिट कार्ड] लेते हैं?

1214. May I pay with a personal check?

kyaa main chék dé [sak-taa (M.)] [sak-tee (F.)] hoon? क्या मैं चेक दे [सकता] [सकती] हूँ?

1215. Will you accept this identification?

kyaa aap yé pa-ri-chay svee-kaar ka-rén-gé? क्या आप यह परिचय स्वीकार करेंगे?

1216. Is the letter of reference sufficient?

kyaa yé pra-maaN-pa-tra kaa-fee hai?

क्या यह प्रमाणपत्र काफ़ी है?

1217. Can you send it to my hotel?

kyaa aap i-sé mé-ré ho-Tal bhéj-vaa sak-té hain?

क्या आप इसे मेरे होटल भेजवा सकते हैं?

1218. Can you ship it [to New York City]?

kyaa i-sé ja-haaz sé [nyoo yaark] bhéj sak-té hain?

क्या इसे जहाज़ से [न्यू यार्क] भेज सकते हैं?

1219. Pack this carefully for export.

i-sé vi-désh bhéj-né ké li-yé saav-dhaa-nee sé paik kee-ji-yé.

इसे विदेश भेजने के लिये सावधानी से पैक कीजिये।

1220. Give me [a bill].

mu-jhé [bil] dee-ji-yé.   मुझे [बिल] दीजिये।

1221. —a receipt.

—ra-seed.   — रसीद।

1222. —a credit memo.

—ja-maa-pa-tra.   — जमापत्र।

1223. I shall pay upon delivery.

main chhu-Raa-ee par pai-sé [doon-gaa (M.)] [doon-gee (F.)].

मैं छुड़ाई पर पैसे [दूंगा] [दूंगी]।

1224. Is there an additional charge for delivery?

kyaa bhéj-né ké a-lag pai-sé la-gén-gé?

क्या भेजने के अलग पैसे लगेंगे?

1225. I wish to return this article.

maiṅ yé cheez lau-Taa-naa [chaa-ha-taa (M.)] [chaa-ha-tee (F.)] hoon.

मैं यह चीज़ लौटाना [चाहता] [चाहती] हूं।

1226. Refund my money.

mu-jhé pai-sé lau-Ta dee-ji-yé. मुझे पैसे लौटा दीजिये।

1227. Please exchange this.

i-sé ba-dal dee-ji-yé. इसे बदल दीजिये।

CLOTHING AND ACCESSORIES

1228. A bathing cap.

ra-baR kee To-pee. रबड़ की टोपी।

1229. A bathing suit.

svi-ming kaus-Tyoom. स्विमिंग कौस्ट्यूम।

1230. A belt.

pé-Tee. पेटी।

1231. A blouse.

cho-lee. चोली।

1232. Boots.

joo-té (OR: booT). जूते (बूट)।

1233. Bangles.

choo-Ri-yaan. चूड़ियां।

1234. Bracelet.

kan-gan. कंगन।

1235. Brassiere.

baa-Dee. बाडी।

1236. Briefs.
jaan-ghi-yaa.   जाँघिया ।

1237. A button.
ba-Tan.   बटन ।

1238. A cane.
chha-Ree.   छड़ी ।

1239. A cap.
To-pee.   टोपी ।

1240. A coat.
koT.   कोट ।

1241. A collar.
kaa-lar.   कालर ।

1242. Cufflinks.
aas-teen ké ba-Tan.   आस्तीन के बटन ।

1243. A dress.
fraak.   फ़्राक ।

1244. Earrings.
jhum-ké (OR: baa-li-yaan).   झुमके (बालियाँ) ।

1245. Gloves.
das-taa-né.   दस्ताने ।

1246. A handbag.
ba-Tu-aa.   बटुआ ।

1247. Handkerchief.
roo-maal.   रूमाल ।

1248. A jacket.
jaa-kéT.   जाकेट ।

1249. A dinner jacket.
jodh-pu-ree koT (OR: Di-nar jai-kéT).
जोधपुरी कोट (डिनर जाकेट) ।

1250. Lingerie.
an-dar ké kap-Ré.   अन्दर के कपड़े ।

1251. A necktie.
Taa-ee.   टाई ।

1252. A nightgown.
so-né kee po-shaak.   सोने की पोशाक ।

1253. Pajamas (Western-style).
so-né ké kap-Ré (OR: naa-iT sooT).
सोने के कपड़े (नाइट सूट) ।

1254. Pajamas (Indian-style trousers).
pai-jaa-maa.   पैजामा ।

1255. Panties.
jaan-ghi-yaa.   जांघिया ।

1256. A pin (decorative).
broch (OR: kaan-Taa).   ब्रोच (कांटा) ।

1257. A safety pin.
su-ra-kshaa-pin.   सुरक्षा-पिन ।

1258. A straight pin.
aal-peen.   आलपीन ।

1259. A raincoat.
bar-saa-tee.   बरसाती ।

1260. Ribbon.
fee-taa.   फ़ीता ।

1261. A ring.
an-goo-THee. अँगूठी ।

1262. Rubbers.
gam booT. गम बूट ।

1263. Sandals.
chap-pal. चप्पल ।

1264. A sari (wrapped woman's dress).
saa-Ree. साड़ी ।

1265. A sarong (worn by men).
lun-gee. लुँगी ।

1266. A man's sash.
ka-mar-band. कमरबन्द ।

1267. A woman's sash.
kar-dha-nee. करधनी ।

1268. A lady's scarf.
du-paT-Taa. दुपटटा ।

1269. A man's scarf.
gu-loo-band. गुलूबन्द ।

1270. A shawl.
shaal. शाल ।

1271. A shirt (Indian-style).
kur-taa. कुरता ।

1272. A shirt (Western-style).
ka-meez. कमीज़ ।

1273. Shoelaces.
fee-té. फ़ीते ।

1274. Shoes.
joo-té.   जूते ।

1275. Shoulderbag.
thé-laa.   थैला ।

1276. Slippers.
chaT-Tee (OR: chap-pal).   चटटी (चप्पल) ।

1277. Socks.
mo-zé.   मोज़े ।

1278. Walking shorts.
ni-kar.   निकर ।

1279. A skirt (long Indian).
la-hén-gaa.   लहँगा ।

1280. A skirt (Western-style).
skarT.   स्कर्ट ।

1281. A slip.
pé-Tee-koT (OR: saa-yaa).   पेटीकोट (साया) ।

1282. Stockings.
lam-bé mo-zé.   लम्बे मोज़े ।

1283. A strap.
paT-Ta.   पटटा ।

1284. A man's suit.
sooT.   सूट ।

1285. A woman's suit.
sal-vaar-ka-meez.   सलवार-कमीज़ ।

1286. A sweater.
ga-ram jar-see.   गरम जरसी ।

1287. A pair of trousers.
pat-loon. पतलून ।

1288. Indian trousers (tight-fitting, worn by both men and women).
choo-Ree-daar pai-jaa-maa. चूड़ीदार पैजामा ।

1289. An umbrella.
chhaa-taa. छाता ।

1290. An undershirt.
ban-yaan. बनयान ।

1291. Undershorts.
kach-chhaa. कच्छा ।

1292. A wallet.
ba-Tu-aa. बटुआ ।

COLORS

1293. Black.
kaa-laa. कालT ।

1294. [Light] [Dark] [Medium] blue.
[hal-kaa] [géh-raa] [ma-dhyam] nee-laa.
[हल्का] [गहरा] [मध्यम] नीला ।

1295. Brown.
bhoo-raa. भूरा ।

1296. Green.
ha-raa. हरा ।

1297. Grey.
dhun-dha-laa. धुन्धला ।

1298. Olive green (OR: **Khaki**).
*kh*aa-kee. ख़ाकी ।

1299. Orange.
naa-ran-gee kaa rang. नारंगी का रंग ।

1300. Pink.
gu-laa-bee. गुलाबी ।

1301. Purple.
bain-ga-nee. बैंगनी ।

1302. Red.
laal. लाल ।

1303. Tan.
hal-kaa bhoo-raa. हलका भूरा ।

1304. White.
sa-féd. सफ़ेद ।

1305. Yellow.
pee-laa. पीला ।

MATERIALS

1306. Metal.
dhaa-tu. धातु ।

1307. Aluminum.
ai-lu-min-yam. ऐलुमिनियम ।

1308. Brass.
pee-tal. पीतल ।

1309. Copper.
taam-baa. तांबा ।

1310. Gold.
so-naa. सोना ।

1311. Iron.
lo-haa. लोहा ।

1312. Silver.
chāan-dee. चाँदी ।

1313. Steel.
i-sTeel (OR: is-paat).
इस्टील (इस्पात) ।

1314. Textiles.
kap-Raa. कपड़ा ।

1315. Cotton [cloth].
soo-tee [kap-Raa]. सूती [कपड़ा] ।

1316. Hand-woven cotton.
khaa-dee. खादी ।

1317. Dacron.
Dai-kraan. डैक्रान ।

1318. Nylon.
naa-i-laan. नाइलान ।

1319. Orlon.
aur-laan. औरलान ।

1320. Silk.
ré-sham. रेशम ।

1321. Wool.
oon. ऊन ।

1322. Ceramics.
chee-nee miT-Tee. चीनी मिट्टी ।

1323. China.
chee-nee ké bar-tan. चीनी के बरतन ।

1324. Crystal.
bil-laur. बिल्लौर ।

1325. Fur.
lom. लोम ।

1326. Gems.
na-gee-né. नगीने ।

1327. Glass.
kaanch. कांच ।

1328. Leather.
cham-Raa. चमड़ा ।

1329. Stone.
pat-thar. पत्थर ।

1330. Wood.
lak-Ree. लकड़ी ।

BOOKSHOP, STATIONER & NEWSDEALER

1331. Do you have any [books] in English?
kyaa aap ké paas an-gré-zee [ki-taa-bén] hain?
क्या आप के पास औग्रेज़ी [किताबें] है ?

1332. I am just browsing.
main yoon-heen dékh [ra-haa (M.)] [ra-hee (F.)] hoon.
मैं यूंही देख [रहा] [रही] हूं।

1333. Playing cards.
taash. ताश ।

1334. A dictionary.
shab-da-kosh. शब्दकोश ।

1335. A dozen envelopes.
ék dar-jan li-faa-fé. एक दर्जन लिफ़ाफ़े।

1336. An eraser.
ra-bar. रबर ।

1337. Fiction.
ka-thaa-saa-hit-ya. कथा-साहित्य ।

1338. Folders.
faa-il ka-var. फ़ाइल कवर ।

1339. A guidebook.
gaa-iD-buk (OR: pra-dar-shi-kaa).
गाइडबुक (प्रदर्शिका) ।

1340. Ink.
syaa-hee. स्याही ।

1341. A map.
naq-shaa. नक़्शा ।

1342. Any magazines.
ko-ee pa-tri-kaa. कोई पत्रिका ।

1343. A newspaper.
akh-baar (OR: sa-maa-chaar-pa-tra).
अख़बार (समाचारपत्र) ।

1344. A notebook.
kaa-pee. कापी ।

1345. Novels.
naa-vil. नाविल ।

1346. Airmail stationery.
ha-vaa-ee Daak ké kaa-*ghaz* aur li-faa-fé.
हवाई डाक के कागज़ और लिफ़ाफ़े।

1347. Carbon paper.
kaar-ban. कारबन।

1348. Writing paper.
kaa-*ghaz*. कागज़।

1349. A fountain pen.
ka-lam. कलम।

1350. A ballpoint pen.
baal-pén. बालपेन।

1351. A pencil.
pén-sil. पेंसिल।

1352. Tape.
Tép. टेप।

1353. Scotch tape.
chi-pak-né vaa-lee Tép (OR: sé-lo-Tép).
चिपकने वाली टेप (सेलोटेप)।

1354. String.
sut-lee. सुतली।

1355. A typewriter.
Taa-ip-raa-i-Tar. टाइपराइटर।

1356. Typewriter ribbon.
Taa-ip-raa-i-Tar ri-ban. टाइपराइटर रिबन।

1357. Wrapping paper.
sa-jaa-va-Tee kaa-*ghaz*. सजावटी कागज़।

PHARMACY*

1358. Is there a [pharmacy] here where they understand English?

ya-haan ko-ee [da-vaa-khaa-naa] hai ja-haan ko-ee an-gré-zee sa-majh-taa ho?

यहाँ कोई [दवाख़ाना] है जहाँ कोई अँग्ज़ी समझता हो?

1359. May I speak to [a male clerk] [a female clerk]?

kyaa main [baa-boo-jee] [ba-hén-jee]† sé baat kar [sak-taa (M.)] [sak-tee (F.)] hoon?

क्या मैं [बाबूजी] [बहनजी] से बात कर [सकता] [सकती] हूँ?

1360. Can you fill this prescription [immediately]?

kyaa yé nus-khaa [tu-rant] bhar sak-té hain?

क्या यह नुस्ख़ा [तुरन्त] भर सकते हैं?

1361. Is [the medication] mild?

[da-vaa] hal-kee hai na?   [दवा] हल्की है न?

1362. Antibiotic.

ain-Tee-baa-yaa-Tik.   ऐन्टीबायाटिक।

1363. Sleeping pill.

neend kee go-lee (OR: svaa-pak da-vaa).

नीन्द की गोली (स्वापक दवा)।

1364. Tranquilizer.

shaa-mak.   शामक।

---

* Doctors and pharmacists operate bilingually. You may use English if the disease is complicated to avoid misunderstanding.

† This is the word for sister but it is used generally for all female workers that one would encounter; it is polite and customary.

1365. Caution!
saav-dhaan! सावधान ।

1366. Poison.
za-hér (OR: vish). ज़हर (विष) ।

1367. Take according to directions.
nir-dé-shaa-nu-saar lee-ji-yé. निर्देशानुसार लीजिये ।

1368. Not to be taken internally.
aan-ta-rik up-bhog ké li-yé na-heen hai.
आन्तरिक उपभोग के लिये नहीं है ।

1369. For external use only.
ké-val baa-ha-ree pra-yog ké li-yé.
केवल बाहरी प्रयोग के लिये ।

DRUGSTORE ITEMS

1370. Adhesive tape.
chi-pak-né vaa-lee Tép. चिपकने वाली टेप ।

1371. Aftershave lotion.
ha-jaa-mat kaa lo-shan. हजामत का लोशन ।

1372. Alcohol.
spi-riT. स्पिरिट ।

1373. Aspirin.
sar dard kee ti-ki-yaa (OR: ais-pro).
सर दर्द की टिकिया (ऐस्प्रो) ।

1374. Antiseptic.
ain-Tee-sép-Tik (OR: Di-Taal). ऐंटीसेप्टिक (डिटाल) ।

1375. Band-Aid.
i-laas-To-plaasT. इलास्टोप्लास्ट ।

1376. Bandages.
paT-Tee. पट्टी ।

1377. Massage oil.
maa-lish kaa tél. मालिश का तेल ।

1378. Bicarbonate of soda.
so-Daa baa-ee kaarb. सोडा बाई कार्ब ।

1379. Bobby pin (OR: Hair pin).
chim-Tee (OR: baal kaa kāan-Taa).
चिमटी (बाल का कांटा) ।

1380. Boric acid.
bo-rik paa-u-Dar. बोरिक पाउडर ।

1381. Chewing gum.
choo-ing gam. चूईंग गम ।

1382. Box of cleansing tissues.
Ti-shoo kaa Dab-baa. टिशू का डब्बा ।

1383. Cold cream.
shee-tal kreem. शीतल क्रीम ।

1384. Comb.
kan-ghee. कंघी ।

1385. Compact.
chéh-ré ké paa-u-Dar kaa Dib-baa.
चेहरे के पाउडर का डिब्बा ।

1386. Contraceptives.
garbh-ro-dhak. गर्भरोधक ।

1387. Corn pad.
ghaT-THé kee paT-Tee. घट्ठे की पट्टी ।

1388. Cotton (absorbent).
roo-ee. रुई ।

1389. Cough syrup.
kh$\overline{aan}$-see kee da-vaa. खाँसी की दवा ।

1390. Deodorant.
dur-gandh-har. दुर्गन्धहर ।

1391. Depilatory.
vi-mo-lan. विमोलन ।

1392. Disinfectant.
ro-gaa-Nu-naa-shak. रोगाणुनाशक ।

1393. Earplug.
TH$\overline{en}$-THee. ठेंठी ।

1394. Enema bag.
a-nee-maa. अनीमा ।

1395. Eye cup.
$\overline{aankh}$ dho-né kaa pyaa-laa. आँख धोने का प्याला ।

1396. Eyewash.
$\overline{aankh}$ dho-né kee da-vaa (OR: né-tra-dhaa-van).
आँख धोने की दवा (नेत्र-धावन) ।

1397. Gauze.
paT-Tee kaa kap-Raa. पट्टी का कपड़ा ।

1398. Hairbrush.
baa-l$\overline{on}$ kaa brash. बालों का ब्रश ।

1399. Hair clip.
klip. क्लिप ।

1400. Hair net.
joo-Ré kee jaa-lee. जूड़े की जाली ।

1401. (Scented) Hair oil.
(su-gan-dhit) baal kaa tél. (सुगंधित) बाल का तेल ।

1402. Hair tonic.
hé-yar Dré-sing. हेयर ड्रेसिंग ।

1403. Hairspray.
hé-yar spré. हेयर स्प्रे ।

1404. Hand lotion.
haath kaa lo-shan. हाथ का लोशन ।

1405. Hot-water bottle.
ga-ram paa-nee kee bo-tal. गरम पानी की बोतल ।

1406. Ice bag.
barf kee thai-lee. बर्फ़ की थैली ।

1407. Insecticide.
kee-Taa-Nu-naa-shak (OR: fliT). कीटाणुनाशक (फ्लिट) ।

1408. Iodine.
aa-yo-Deen. आयोडीन ।

1409. Laxative.
ju-laab. जुलाब ।

1410. Lipstick.
lip-sTik. लिपस्टिक ।

1411. Medicine dropper.
Draa-par. ड्रापर ।

1412. Mirror.
shee-shaa. शीशा ।

1413. Mouthwash.
kul-laa kar-né kee da-vaa (OR: mukh-dhaa-van).
कुल्ला करने की दवा (मुख-धावन) ।

1414. Nail file.
naa-*khoon*-ré-tee. नाख़ून-रेती ।

1415. Nail polish.
naa-*khoon* kee paa-lish. नाख़ून की पालिश ।

1416. Nose drops.
naak kee da-vaa. नाक की दवा ।

1417. Ointment.
mar-ham. मरहम ।

1418. Peroxide.
haa-ee-Dro-jan pé-rok-saa-eeD. हाईड्रोजन पेरोक्साईड ।

1419. [Face] [Foot] [Talcum] powder.
[chéh-ré kaa] [pair kaa] [Taal-kam] paa-u-Dar.
[चेहरे का] [पैर का] [टालकम] पाउडर ।

1420. Powder puff.
ga-di-yaa. गदिया ।

1421. Straight razor.
dé-shee us-traa. देशी उस्तरा ।

1422. Electric razor.
bij-lee kaa us-traa. बिजली का उस्तरा ।

1423. Safety razor.
us-traa. उस्तरा ।

1424. Razor blade.
bléD. ब्लेड ।

1425. Rouge.
laa-lee. लाली ।

1426. Sanitary napkins.
sai-ni-Tree Taa-val. सैनिट्री टावल ।

1427. Sedative.
neend kee da-vaa (OR: shaa-mak).
नींद की दवा (शामक)।

1428. Shampoo.
baal dho-né kaa saa-bun. बाल धोने का साबुन।

1429. Shaving brush.
ha-jaa-mat brash. हजामत ब्रश।

1430. Shaving cream.
ha-jaa-mat ba-naa-né kee kreem.
हजामत बनाने की क्रीम।

1431. Shaving lotion.
ha-jaa-mat kaa lo-shan. हजामत का लोशन।

1432. Shower cap.
na-haa-né kee To-pee. नहाने की टोपी।

1433. Soap.
saa-bun. साबुन।

1434. Sponge.
spanj. स्पंज।

1435. Sunburn ointment.
dhoop-taa-mar kee mar-ham.
धूपताम् की मरहम।

1436. Sunglasses.
dhoop-chash-maa. धूपचश्मा।

1437. Suntan oil (OR: **lotion**).
dhoop tél. धूप तेल।

1438. Syringe.
soo-ee. सूई।

1439. Tampons.
Taim-paan (OR: piks). टैम्पान (पिक्स)।

1440. Thermometer [centigrade] [fahrenheit].
thar-maa-mee-Tar [sén-Tee-gréD] [fai-ran-haa-iT].
थर्मामीटर [सेन्टीग्रेड] [फ़ैरनहाइट]।

1441. Toothbrush.
daant brash. दाँत ब्रश।

1442. Toothpaste.
dant man-jan. दन्त मंजन।

1443. Toothpowder.
dant paa-u-Dar. दन्त पाउडर।

1444. Vaseline.
vais-leen. वैसलीन।

1445. Vitamins.
vi-Taa-min. विटामिन।

CAMERA SHOP AND PHOTOGRAPHY

1446. I want a roll of film [for this camera].
mu-jhé [is kaim-ré ké li-yé] ék film chaa-hi-yé.
मुझे [इस कैमरे के लिये] एक फ़िल्म चाहिये।

1447. Do you have [color film]?
aap ké paas [ran-geen film] hai?
आप के पास [रंगीन फ़िल्म] है?

1448. —black-and-white film.
—saa-dee film. _ सादी फ़िल्म।

1449. —movie film.

—chal-chi-tra film. _ चलचित्र फ़िल्म ।

1450. What is the charge [for developing a roll]?

[film dhul-vaa-né kaa] kyaa daam hai?

[फ़िल्म धुलवाने का] क्या दाम है?

1451. —for enlarging.

—tas-veer ba-Ree kar-vaa-né kaa.

_ तस्वीर बड़ी करवाने का ।

1452. —for one print.

—ék fo-To kaa. _ एक फ़ोटो का ।

1453. May I take a photo of you?

main aap kee tas-veer kheench [sak-taa (M.)] [sak-tee (F.)] hoon?

मैं॰ आप की तस्वीर खींच [सकता] [सकती] हूं?

1454. Would you take a photo of me, please?

za-raa aap mé-ree tas-veer kheench dee-ji-yé.

ज़रा आप मेरी तस्वीर खींच दीजिये ।

1455. A color print.

ran-geen tas-veer. रंगीन तस्वीर ।

1456. Flashbulb.

kaundh-balb. कौंध-बल्ब ।

1457. The lens.

léns. लेन्स ।

1458. The negative.

ni-gé-tiv (OR: pra-ti-chi-tra).

निगेटिव (प्रतिचित्र) ।

1459. The shutter.

sha-Tar. शतर ।

1460. A transparency (OR: slide).
paar-dar-shee chi-tra (OR: slaa-iD).

पारदर्शी चित्र (स्लाइड) ।

1461. A tripod.
ti-paa-ee. तिपाई ।

GIFT AND SOUVENIR LIST

1462. Basket.
Tok-ree. टोकरी ।

1463. Box of candy.
mi-THaa-ee kaa Dab-baa. मिठाई का डब्बा ।

1464. Doll.
gu-Ri-yaa. गुड़िया ।

1465. Embroidery.
ka-shee-daa-kaa-ree. कशीदाकारी ।

1466. Handicrafts.
hast-ka-laa. हस्तकला ।

1467. Jewelry.
zé-var (OR: géh-né). ज़ेवर (गहने) ।

1468. Lace.
fee-taa. फ़ीता ।

1469. Needlework.
ka-shee-daa. कशीदा ।

1470. Penknife.
chho-Taa chaa-koo (OR: ka-lam-ta-raash).
छोटा चाकू (कलमतराश) ।

1471. Perfume.
i-tar. इत्र ।

1472. Phonograph records.
ri-kaarD. रिकार्ड ।

1473. Pottery.
miT-Tee ké bar-tan. मिट्टी के बरतन ।

1474. Precious stones.
na-gee-né. नगीने ।

1475. Print (graphic).
chha-pee tas-veer. छपी तस्वीर ।

1476. Souvenir.
ni-shaa-nee (OR: yaad-gaar). निशानी (यादगार) ।

TOBACCO SHOP

1477. Where is the nearest tobacco shop?
ya-haan paas mén tam-baa-koo kee du-kaan ka-haan hai?
यहाँ पास में तम्बाकू की दुकान कहाँ है?

1478. I want some cigars.
mu-jhé kuchh si-gaar chaa-hi-yé.
मुझे कुछ सिगार चाहिये ।

1479. What brands of cigarettes [with menthol] do you have?
aap ké paas kaun-see chhaap ké [mén-thol] sig-réT hain?
आप के पास कौनसी छाप के [मेन्थोल] सिगेट हैं ?

1480. One pack of king-size [filter-tip] cigarettes.
ék Dib-bee lam-bé [fil-Tar vaa-lé] sig-réT chaa-hi-yé.

एक डिब्बी लम्बे [फ़िल्टर वाले] सिगरेट चाहिये।

1481. I need a lighter.
mu-jhé ja-laa-né vaa-laa chaa-hi-yé.

मुझे जलाने वाला चाहिये।

1482. Lighter fluid.
ja-laa-né vaa-lé kaa ma-saa-laa. जलाने वाले का मसाला।

1483. Flint.
chak-mak. चकमक।

1484. Matches.
di-yaa-sa-laa-ee. दियासलाई।

1485. A pipe.
vi-laa-ya-tee chi-lam (OR: paa-ip).

विलायती चिलम (पाइप)।

1486. Pipe cleaners.
chi-lam saaf kar-né vaa-lee seekh.

चिलम साफ़ करने वाली सींख।

1487. Pipe tobacco.
vi-laa-ya-tee tam-baa-koo. विलायती तम्बाकू।

1488. Tobacco pouch.
tam-baa-koo kee thai-lee. तम्बाकू की थैली।

1489. Water pipe.
huk-kaa. हुक्का।

1490. Chewing tobacco.
tam-baa-koo kee pat-tee. तम्बाकू की पत्ती।

1491. Snuff.
nas-vaar. नसवार ।

1492. Cheroots.
bee-Ree. बीड़ी ।

1493. Betel nut.*
su-paa-ree. सुपारी ।

1494. Plain betel.
saa-daa paan. सादा पान ।

1495. Scented betel nut.
mee-THee su-paa-ree. मीठी सुपारी ।

1496. Sweet betel.
mee-THaa paan. मीठा पान ।

LAUNDRY AND DRY CLEANING

1497. Where can I get my [dirty clothes] washed?
[mai-lé kap-Ré] ka-haan dhul-vaa-é jaa-té hain?

[मैले कपड़े] कहाँ धुलवाए जाते है ?

1498. Is there a dry-cleaning service near here?
kyaa paas mén Draa-ee klee-nar kee du-kaan hai?

क्या पास में ड्राई क्लीनर की दुकान है?

---

* Betel leaves and nuts are sold at tobacco stalls and special stands. They are equivalent to our chewing gum and consist of a betel leaf wrapped around chunks of betel nut, with other flavorings, sweet spices & tobacco. A *paan* is said to freshen the breath and promote digestion.

1499. What day does the washerman come?
dho-bee kaun-sé din aa-taa hai?
धोबी कौनसे दिन आता है?

1500. Wash this blouse in [hot water].
is cho-lee ko [ga-ram paa-nee] mén dho-i-yé-gaa.
इस चोली को [गरम पानी] में धोइयेगा।

1501. —lukewarm water.
kun-ku-né paa-nee. कुनकुने पानी।

1502. —cold water.
—THan-Dé paa-nee. _ ठंडे पानी।

1503. No starch, please.
ka-laf mat la-gaa-i-yé-gaa. कलफ़ मत लगाइयेगा।

1504. Remove the stain [from this shirt].
[is ka-meez sé] yé daagh u-taar dee-ji-yé-gaa.
[इस कमीज़ से] यह दाग़ उतार दीजियेगा।

1505. Press [the trousers].
[pat-loon] is-tree kee-ji-yé. [पतलून] इस्त्री कीजिये।

1506. Starch [the collar].
[kaa-lar] mén ka-laf la-gaa-i-yé. [कालर] में कलफ़
लगाइये।

1507. Dry-clean [this coat].
[is koT] ko Draa-ee kleen kee-ji-yé.
[इस कोट] को ड्राई क्लीन कीजिये।

1508. [The belt] is missing.
[is kee pé-Tee] kam hai. [इस की पेटी] कम है।

1509. Sew on [this button].
[yé ba-Tan] la-gaa dee-ji-yé-gaa. [यह बटन] लगा
दीजियेगा।

REPAIRS AND ADJUSTMENTS

1510. This does not work.
yé kaam na-heen kar-taa. यह काम नहीं करता ।

1511. This watch runs [fast] [slow].
yé gha-Ree [téz] [dhee-ré] chal-tee hai.
यह घड़ी [तेज़] [धीरे] चलती है ।

1512. [My glasses] are broken.
[mé-ree ai-nak] TooT ga-ee. [मेरी ऐनक] टूट गई ।

1513. It is torn.
yé phaT ga-yaa. यह फट गया ।

1514. Where can I get it repaired?
main i-sé ka-haan THeek kar-vaa [sak-taa (M.)] [sak-tee (F.)] hoon?

मैं इसे कहाँ ठीक करवा [सकता] [सकती] हूँ?

1515. Fix [this lock].
[is taa-lé] ko THeek kee-ji-yé.
[इस ताले] को ठीक कीजिये ।

1516. Fix [the sole].
[tal-vé] kee ma-ram-mat kee-ji-yé.
[तलवे] की मरम्मत कीजिये ।

1517. —the heel.
—é-Ree. _ एड़ी ।

1518. —the uppers.
—oo-par kaa hissaa. _ ऊपर का हिस्सा ।

1519. —the strap.
—paT-Tee. _ पट्टी ।

1520. Lengthen [this skirt].
[la-hén-gaa] lam-baa kar dee-ji-yé.

[लहंगा] लम्बा कर दीजिये ।

1521. Shorten [the sleeves].
[aas-tee-nén] chho-Tee kar dee-ji-yé.

[आस्तीनें] छोटी कर दीजिये ।

1522. Replace [the lining].
[aas-tar] ba-dal dee-ji-yé.   [आस्तर] बदल दीजिये ।

1523. Sew [the pocket].
[jéb] see dee-ji-yé.   [जेब] सी दीजिये ।

1524. Fasten it together.
in-hén joR dee-ji-yé.   इन्हें जोड़ दीजिये ।

1525. Clean [the mechanism].
[yan-tra] saaf kee-ji-yé.   [यंत्र] साफ़ कीजिये ।

1526. Lubricate [the spring].
[ka-maa-nee] kee gree-sing kar dee-ji-yé.

[कमानी] की ग्रीसिंग कर दीजिये ।

1527. Needle.
soo-ee.   सूई ।

1528. Scissors.
kain-chee.   कैंची ।

1529. Thimble.
an-gush-taa-naa.   अंगुश्ताना ।

1530. Thread.
dhaa-gaa.   धागा ।

BARBER SHOP

1531. Give me a haircut, please.
baal kaaT dee-ji-yé. बाल काट दीजिये।

1532. Just a trim.
baal tho-Ré chho-Té kar dee-ji-yé.
बाल थोड़े छोटे कर दीजिये।

1533. Give me [a shave].
[ha-jaa-mat] ba-naa dee-ji-yé. [हजामत] बना दीजिये।

1534. Give me a shoeshine.
joo-té paa-lish kar dee-ji-yé. जूते पालिश कर दीजिये।

1535. Don't cut too much hair [off the top] [on the sides].
[oo-par ké] [ba-ghal ké] baal zyaa-daa na-heen kaa-Ti-yé-
    gaa.
[ऊपर के] [बग़ल के] बाल ज्यादा नहीं काटियेगा।

1536. I want to keep my hair long.
mu-jhé baal lam-bé rakh-né hain.
मुझे बाल लम्बे रखने हैं।

1537. I part my hair [on this side].
main maang [is ta-raf] ni-kaal-taa (M.) hoon.
मैं मांग [इस तरफ़] निकालता हूं।

1538. —on the other side.
—doos-ree ta-raf. _ दूसरी तरफ़।

1539. —in the middle.
—beech kee. _ बीच की।

1540. No hair tonic.
tél mat la-gaa-i-yé. तेल मत लगाइये।

1541. Trim [my mustache].
[mé-ree moon-chhén] chho-Tee kar dee-ji-yé.
[मेरी मूँछे] छोटी कर दीजिये।

1542. —my eyebrows.
—mé-ree bhaun-én. मेरी भौंपें।

1543. —my beard.
—mé-ree daa-RHee. मेरी दाढ़ी।

1544. —my sideburns.
—gal-much-chhén. गलमुच्छें।

BEAUTY PARLOR

1545. Can I make an appointment for [Monday afternoon]?
kyaa [som-vaar do-pa-har] kaa sa-may tay kar sak-tee hoon?
क्या [सोमवार दोपहर] का समय तय कर सकती हूँ?

1546. Comb my hair.
kan-ghee kar dee-ji-yé. कंघी कर दीजिये।

1547. Wash my hair.
mé-ré baal dho dee-ji-yé. मेरे बाल धो दीजिये।

1548. Shampoo and set, please.
baal dho kar ba-naa dee-ji-yé.
बाल धो कर बना दीजिये।

1549. Not too short.
ba-hut chho-Té na-heen. बहुत छोटे नहीं।

1550. In this style, please.
i-see DHang kaa. इसी ढंग का।

1551. Dye my hair [in this shade].

baal [is rang mén] rang dee-ji-yé.

बाल [इस रंग में] रंग दीजिये ।

1552. Clean and set this wig.

baa-lon kee To-pee ko saaf kar-ké ba-naa dee-ji-yé.

बालों की टोपी को साफ़ करके बना दीजिये ।

1553. A curl.

ghoon-ghar. घूंघर ।

1554. A facial.

chéh-ré kee sa-faa-ee. चेहरे की सफ़ाई ।

1555. A hairpiece.

naq-lee baal. नक़ली बाल ।

1556. A manicure.

naa-*kh*un ban-vaa-naa. नाख़ुन बनवाना ।

1557. A massage.

maa-lish. मालिश ।

1558. A permanent wave.

par-maa-nénT. परमिनेन्ट ।

STORES AND SERVICES

1559. Antique shop.

praa-cheen vas-tu-on kee du-kaan.

प्राचीन वस्तुओं की दुकान ।

1560. Art gallery.

ka-laa koshTH. कला कोष्ठ ।

1561. Artist's materials.
ka-laa-kaa-ree kee chee-zén. कलाकारी की चीज़ें।

1562. Auto rental.
mo-Tar ki-raa-yé kee du-kaan. मोटर किराये की दुकान।

1563. Auto repairs.
mo-Tar kaar-*khaa*-naa. मोटर कारख़ाना।

1564. Bakery.
naan-baa-ee. नानबाई।

1565. Bank.
baink. बैंक।

1566. Bar.
sha-raab-*khaa*-naa (OR: mai-*khaa*-naa).
शराबख़ाना (मैख़ाना)।

1567. Barber.
naa-ee (OR: haj-jaam). नाई (हज्जाम)।

1568. Beauty salon.
saun-dar-ya pra-saa-dhan kee du-kaan.
सौन्दर्य प्रसाधन की दुकान।

1569. Bookshop.
ki-taab kee du-kaan. किताब की दुकान।

1570. Butcher.
ka-saa-ee. कसाई।

1571. Candy shop.
mi-THaa-ee kee du-kaan. मिठाई की दुकान।

1572. Checkroom.
as-baab-ghar. असबाबघर।

1573. [Children's] [Men's] [Women's] clothing store.
[bach-chõn ké] [aad-mi-yõn ké] [aur-tõn ké] kap-Rõn kee
  du-kaan.
[बच्चों के] [आदमियों के] [औरतों के] कपड़ों की
  दुकान ।

1574. Saree store.
saa-Ree kee du-kaan. साड़ी की दुकान ।

1575. Cosmetics.
shrin-gaar kee vas-tu-ẽn. श्रृंगार की वस्तुएँ ।

1576. Dance studio.
nri-tya sTu-Di-yo. नृत्य स्टुडियो ।

1577. Dentist.
dant-chi-kit-sak (OR: dãant kaa Daak-Tar).
दन्तचिकित्सक (दाँत का डाकटर) ।

1578. Department store.
soo-par baa-zaar. सूपर बाज़ार ।

1579. Drugstore (OR: **Pharmacy**).
da-vaa-khaa-naa. दवाख़ाना ।

1580. Dry cleaners.
Draa-ee klee-nar. ड्राई क्लीनर ।

1581. Electrical supplies.
bij-lee kaa saa-maan. बिजली का सामान ।

1582. Employment agency.
ni-yo-jan kaar-yaa-lay.
नियोजन कार्यालय ।

1583. Fish store.
machh-lee kee du-kaan. मछली की दुकान ।

1584. Florist.
phool-vaa-laa.   फूलवाला ।

1585. Fruit store.
phal kee du-kaan.   फल की दुकान ।

1586. Furniture store.
far-nee-char kee du-kaan.   फ़रनीचर की दुकान ।

1587. Grocery store (for spices, canned goods, etc.).
pan-saa-ree kee du-kaan.   पन्सारी की दुकान ।

1588. Ladies' hairdresser.
késh-pra-saa-dhak.   केशप्रसाधक ।

1589. Men's hairdresser (OR: Barbershop).
naa-ee kee du-kaan.   नाई की दुकान ।

1590. Hardware store.
lo-hé ké saa-maan kee du-kaan.
लोहे के सामान की दुकान ।

1591. Hat shop.
To-pee kee du-kaan.   टोपी की दुकान ।

1592. Housewares.
bar-tan kee du-kaan.   बरतन की दुकान ।

1593. Jewelry store.
jau-ha-ree kee du-kaan.   जौहरी की दुकान ।

1594. Lawyer.
va-keel.   वकील ।

1595. Laundry.
kap-Ré dho-né kee du-kaan.   कपड़े धोने की दुकान ।

1596. Loans.
karz. कर्ज़ ।

1597. Lumberyard.
lak-kaR baa-zaar. लक्कड़ बाज़ार ।

1598. Market.
baa-zaar. बाज़ार ।

1599. Milliner.
To-pee ba-naa-né vaa-laa. टोपी बनाने वाला ।

1600. Money exchange.
pai-sé ba-dal-né kee du-kaan. पैसे बदलने की दुकान ।

1601. Music store.
vaa-dhya-yan-tron̄ kee du-kaan. वाद्ययंत्रों की दुकान ।

1602. Musical instruments.
vaa-dhya-yan-tra. वाद्ययंत्र ।

1603. Newsstand.
akh-baar-vaa-laa. अख़बारवाला ।

1604. Paint store.
rang kee du-kaan. रंग की दुकान ।

1605. Pastry shop.
kék vaa-laa. केक वाला ।

1606. Photographer.
tas-veer kheench-né vaa-laa. तस्वीर खींचने वाला ।

1607. Photography store.
tas-veer kee du-kaan. तस्वीर की दुकान ।

1608. Printing shop.
chhaap-khaa-naa. छापख़ाना ।

1609. Real estate agent.
ma-kaan béch-né vaa-laa ai-jénT. मकान बेचने वाला एजन्ट।

1610. Sewing machine.
si-laa-ee ma-sheen. सिलाई मशीन।

1611. Shoemaker.
mo-chee. मोची।

1612. Shoe store.
joo-té kee du-kaan. जूते की दुकान।

1613. Sightseeing.
sair sa-paa-Taa. सैर सपाटा।

1614. Sign painter.
paTT rang-né vaa-laa. पट्ट रंगने वाला।

1615. Sporting goods.
khél kaa saa-maan. खेल का सामान।

1616. Stockbroker.
saT-Té kaa da-laal. सट्टे का दलाल।

1617. Tailor.
dar-zee. दर्ज़ी।

1618. Toy shop.
khi-lau-né kee du-kaan. खिलौने की दुकान।

1619. Trucking.
Traans-porT vaa-laa. ट्रान्सपोर्ट वाला।

1620. Upholsterer.
so-faa-saaz. सोफ़ासाज़।

1621. Used cars.
pu-raa-nee gaa-Ree. पुरानी गाड़ी।

1622. Vegetable store.

sab-zee kee du-kaan. सब्ज़ी की दुकान ।

1623. Watchmaker.

gha-Ree-saaz. घड़ीसाज़ ।

1624. Wines and liquors.

sha-raab kee du-kaan. शराब की दुकान ।

BABY CARE

1625. I need a reliable babysitter tonight [at 7 o'clock].

mu-jhé aaj shaam [saat ba-jé] ék bha-ro-sé-daar aa-yaa chaa-hi-yé.

मुझे आज शाम [सात बजे] एक भरोसेदार आया चाहिये ।

1626. Call a pediatrician immediately.

ki-see shi-shu-chi-kit-sak (OR: bach-chõn ké Daak-Tar) ko jal-dee bu-laa dee-ji-yé.

किसी शिशुचिकित्सक (बच्चों के डाकटर) को जल्दी बुला दीजिये ।

1627. Give the baby some [milk].

bach-ché ko [doodh] pi-laa dee-ji-yé.

बच्चे को [दूध] पिला दीजिये ।

1628. Feed the baby.

bach-ché ko khaa-naa khi-laa dee-ji-yé.

बच्चे को खाना खिला दीजिये ।

1629. Change the diaper.

naip-kin ba-dal dee-ji-yé. नैपकिन बदल दीजिये ।

1630. Bathe the baby.

bach-ché ko néh-laa dee-ji-yé. बच्चे को नहला दीजिये ।

1631. Put the baby to sleep [in the crib].

bé-bee ko [kha-To-lé mén] su-laa dee-ji-yé.

बेबी को [खटोले में] सुला दीजिये।

1632. Give the baby a pacifier if he cries.

a-gar bach-chaa ro-yé to u-sé choos-nee dé dee-ji-yé.

अगर बच्चा रोये तो उसे चूसनी दे दीजिये।

1633. Do you have an ointment for [diaper rash]?

kyaa aap ké paas [da-do-ré] kee mar-ham hai?

क्या आप के पास [ददोरे] की मरहम है?

1634. Take the baby to the park in the [carriage].

bach-ché ko baa-gee-ché [praim] mén lé jaa-i-yé.

बच्चे को बागीचे [प्रैम] में ले जाइये।

1635. —stroller.

—bach-ché kcc gaa-Ree. _ बच्चे की गाड़ी।

1636. Baby food.

bach-chon ka khaa-naa. बच्चों का खाना।

1637. Baby powder.

bach-ché kaa paa-u-Dar. बच्चे का पाउडर।

1638. Bib.

ga-ti-yaa. गतिया।

1639. Colic.

an-tra-shool. अन्त्रशूल।

1640. Bottles.

bot-lén. बोतलें।

1641. Diapers.

naip-kin. नैपकिन।

1642. Highchair.

oon-chee kur-see. ऊंची कुर्सी।

1643. Nursemaid.
aa-yaa. आया।

1644. Playground.
khél kaa mai-daan. खेल का मैदान।

1645. Playpen.
kha-To-laa. खटोला।

1646. Rattle.
jhun-jhu-naa. झुनझुना।

1647. Toy.
khi-lau-naa. खिलौना।

HEALTH AND ILLNESS

1648. Is the doctor [at home] [in his office]?
kyaa Daak-Tar saa-hab [ghar par] [daf-tar men] hain?
क्या डाकटर साहब [घर पर] [द्फ़तर में] है॰?

1649. What are his office hours (LIT. When is he in his office)?
vo daf-tar men kab réh-té hain?
वह द्फ़तर में कब रहते है॰?

1650. Take my temperature.
za-raa bu-khaar dé-khi-yé. ज़रा बुख़ार देखिये।

1651. I have something [in my eye].
[mé-ree aankh men] kuchh hai. [मेरी आंख में] कुछ है।

1652. I have a pain [in my back].
[mé-ree peeTH men] dard hai. [मेरी पीठ में] दर्द है।

1653. [My toe] is swollen.

[mé-ré pair kaa an-goo-THaa] sooj ga-yaa hai.

[मेरे पैर का अँगूठा] सूज गया है।

1654. It is sensitive to pressure.

da-baa-né par dard ho-taa hai. दबाने पर दर्द होता है।

1655. Is it serious?

chin-taa vaa-lee baat to na-heen?

चिन्ता वाली बात तो नहीं?

1656. I do not sleep well.

main ach-chhee ta-rah na-heen [so-taa (M.)] [so-tee (F.)].

मैं अच्छी तरह नहीं [सोता] [सोती]।

1657. I have no appetite.

mu-jhé bhook na-heen lag-tee. मुझे भूक नहीं लगती।

1658. Can you give me something for the pain?

mu-jhé dard kee da-vaa dee-ji-yé.

मुझे दर्द की दवा दीजिये।

1659. I am allergic to [penicillin].

mu-jhé [pé-ni-ci-lin] sé é-lar-jee hai.

मुझे [पेनिसिलिन] से एलर्जी है।

1660. Where should I have this prescription filled?

main yé nus-khaa ka-haan bhar-vaa-oon?

मैं यह नुस्ख़ा कहाँ भरवाऊँ?

1661. Do I have to go to [a hospital]?

kyaa mu-jhé [as-pa-taal] jaa-naa pa-Ré-gaa?

क्या मुझे [अस्पताल] जाना पड़ेगा?

1662. Is an operation necessary?

kyaa aap-ré-shan aa-vash-yak hai?

क्या आपरेशन आवश्यक है?

1663. Do I have to stay in bed?

kyaa mu-jhé lé-Té réh-naa ho-gaa?

क्या मुझे लेटे रहना होगा?

1664. When will my health improve?

mé-ree ta-bee-yat ach-chhee kab ho-gee?

मेरी तबीयत अच्छी कब होगी?

1665. Is it a contagious disease?

yé chhoot kee bee-maa-ree to na-heen?

यह छूत की बीमारी तो नहीं?

1666. I feel [better].

mé-ree ta-bee-yat [péh-lé sé zyaa-daa ach-chhee] hai.

मेरी तबीयत [पहले से ज़्यादा अच्छी] है।

1667. —worse.

—péh-lé sé zyaa-daa *kha*-raab. _ पहले से ज़्यादा खराब

1668. —about the same.

—vai-sé hee. _ वैसे ही।

1669. Shall I keep it bandaged?

kyaa main paT-Tee ban-dhee réh-né doon?

क्या मैं पटटी बंधी रहने दूं?

1670. Can I travel [on Monday]?

kyaa main [som-vaar ko] sa-far kar [sak-taa (M.)] [sak-tee (F.)] hoon?

क्या मैं [सोमवार को] सफ़र कर [सकता] [सकती] हूं?

1671. When will you come again?

aap phir kab aa-yen-gé? आप फिर कब आयेंगे?

1672. When should I take the medicine?

main da-vaa kab loon? मैं दवा कब लूं?

1673. When do I get [the injection]?
[Tee-kaa] kab lag-vaa-oon? [टीका] कब लगवाऊँ?

1674. When should I take [the pills]?
main [go-li-yaan] kab khaa-oon?
मैं [गोलियाँ] कब खाऊँ?

1675. Every hour.
har ghan-Té ké baad. हर घंटे के बाद।

1676. [Before] [After] eating.
khaa-né ké [péh-lé] [baad]. खाने के [पहले] [बाद]।

1677. At bedtime.
so-né ké sa-may. सोने के समय।

1678. On getting up.
uTH-né ké sa-may. उठने के समय।

1679. Twice a day.
din mén do baar. दिन में दो बार।

1680. An anesthetic.
bé-ho-shee kee da-vaa. बेहोशी की दवा।

1681. Convalescence.
svaasth-ya-laabh. स्वास्थ्य-लाभ।

1682. Cure.
i-laaj. इलाज।

1683. Diet.
path-ya. पथ्य।

1684. A drop.
ék boond. एक बूँद।

1685. Nurse.
daa-ee. दाई।

1686. Oculist.
né-tra-chi-kit-sak (OR: aankh kaa Daak-Tar).
नेत्र-चिकित्सक (आँख का डाकटर) ।

1687. An orthopedist.
haD-Di-yon̄ kaa Daak-Tar. हड्डियों का डाकटर ।

1688. Remedy.
i-laaj (OR: da-vaa). इलाज (दवा) ।

1689. A specialist.
vi-shé-sha-gya. विशेषज्ञ ।

1690. A surgeon.
sar-jan. सर्जन ।

1691. Treatment.
i-laaj. इलाज ।

1692. X-ray.
éks-ré. एक्स-रे ।

AILMENTS

1693. An abscess.
ma-vaad vaa-laa dān̄t. मवाद वाला दांत ।

1694. An allergy.
é-lar-jee. एलर्जी ।

1695. Asthma.
da-maa. दमा ।

1696. An insect bite.
kee-Ré kaa kaaT-naa. कीड़े का काटना ।

1697. A blister.
chhaa-laa. छाला ।

1698. A boil.
pho-Raa. फोड़ा ।

1699. A bruise.
choT. चोट ।

1700. A burn.
jal-naa. जलना ।

1701. Chicken pox.
ché-chak. चेचक ।

1702. A chill.
joo-Ree. जूड़ी ।

1703. Cholera.
hai-zaa. हैज़ा ।

1704. A cold.
zu-kaam. जुकाम ।

1705. Constipation.
kabz. कब्ज ।

1706. A corn.
ghaT-THaa. घट्ठा ।

1707. A cough.
khaan-see. खाँसी ।

1708. A cramp.
ain-THan (OR: ma-roR). ऐंठन (मरोड़) ।

1709. A cut.
ghaa-o. घाव ।

1710. Diabetes.
ba-hu-moo-tra. बहुमूत्र ।

1711. Diarrhoea.
dast. दस्त ।

1712. Dysentery.
pé-chish. पेचिश ।

1713. Earache.
kaan kaa dard. कान का दर्द ।

1714. Epidemic.
ma-haa-maa-ree. महामारी ।

1715. To feel faint.
chak-kar aa-naa. चक्कर आना ।

1716. Fever.
jvar (OR: bu-*kh*aar). ज्वर (बुख़ार) ।

1717. Fracture.
haD-Dee TooT-naa. हड्डी टूटना ।

1718. Headache.
sar-dard. सरदर्द ।

1719. Hemorrhoids.
ba-vaa-seer. बवासीर ।

1720. Indigestion.
a-pach (OR: bad-haz-mee). अपच (बदहज़मी) ।

1721. Infection.
san-kra-maN. संक्रमण ।

1722. Inflammation.
ja-lan. जलन ।

1723. Influenza.
floo (OR: mo-tee-jha-raa). फ़्लू (मोतीझरा) ।

1724. Insomnia.
a-ni-draa. अनिद्रा ।

1725. Measles.
khas-raa. खसरा ।

1726. Mumps.
kan-pé-Raa. कनपेड़ा ।

1727. Nausea.
mat-lee (OR: au-kaa-ee). मतली (औकाई) ।

1728. Nosebleed.
nak-seer. नक्सीर ।

1729. Poisoning.
vi-shaakt-taa. विषाक्तता ।

1730. Smallpox.
ba-Ree maa-taa. बड़ी माता ।

1731. Snakebite.
sarp-dansh. सर्पदंश ।

1732. Sore throat.
gal-shoth. गलशोथ ।

1733. Sprain.
moch. मोच ।

1734. Bee sting.
ma-dhu-mak-khee kaa kaaT-naa. मधुमक्खी का काटना ।

1735. Sunburn.
dhoop sé jal-naa (OR: dhoop taa-mar-taa).
धूप से जलना (धूप तामृता) ।

1736. Sunstroke.
loo lag-naa. लू लगना ।

1737. Swelling.
soo-jan. सूजन ।

1738. Tonsilitis.
Taan-sil pak-naa. टान्सिल पकना ।

1739. Toothache.
daant kaa dard. दांत का दर्द ।

1740. To vomit.
ul-Tee kar-naa. उलटी करना ।

DENTIST

1741. Can you recommend a [good dentist]?
kyaa aap ki-see [ach-chhé dant-chi-kit-sak] kaa naam ba-taa sak-té hain?

क्या आप किसी [अच्छे दन्तचिकित्सक] का नाम बता सकते है ?

1742. [My filling] has come out.
[mé-ré daant kee bha-raa-ee] ni-kal ga-ee hai.

[मेरे दांत की भराई] निकल गई है ।

1743. Can you replace the filling?
kyaa aap daant do-baa-raa bhar sak-té hain?

क्या आप दांत दोबारा भर सकते है ?

1744. Can you fix [this broken tooth]?
kyaa aap [yé Too-Tee hu-ee daant] la-gaa dén-gé?

क्या आप [यह टूटी हुई दांत] लगा देंगे?

1745. —this denture.
—yé naq-lee daant.   यह नकली दांत ।

1746. I have a toothache.
mé-ré daant mén dard hai.   मेरे दांत में दर्द है ।

1747. My gums are sore.

mé-ré ma-soo-Ré dukh-té hain. मेरे मसूड़े दुखते है' ।

1748. Please [clean] my teeth.

mé-ré daant [saaf kee-ji-yé]. मेरे दांत [साफ़ कीजिये] ।

1749. I have a cavity.

mé-ré daant men kee-Raa lag ga-yaa.

मेरे दांत में कीड़ा लग गया ।

1750. Please give me [a general anesthetic] [a local anesthetic].

mu-jhé [poo-ree bé-ho-shee kee da-vaa] [yé ja-gah sun kar-né kee da-vaa] dee-ji-yé.

मुझे [पूरी बेहोशी की दवा] [यह जगह सुन करने की दवा] दीजिये ।

1751. I [do not] want the tooth extracted.

mu-jhé daant [na-heen] ni-kal-vaa-naa hai.

मुझे दांत [नहीं] निकलवाना है ।

1752. A temporary filling.

kaam-cha-laa-oo bhar-vaa-ee.

कामचलाऊ भरवाई ।

ACCIDENTS

1753. There has been an accident.

ya-haan dur-ghaT-naa ho ga-ee. यहाँ दुर्घटना हो गई ।

1754. Call [a doctor] immediately.

[Daak-Tar] ko tu-rant bu-laa-i-yé. [डाकटर] को तुरन्त बुलाइये ।

1755. —an ambulance.

—as-pa-taal-gaa-Ree. अस्पताल-गाड़ी ।

1756. —a nurse.
—nars. _ नर्स ।

1757. —a policeman.
—pu-lis vaa-laa. _ पुलिस वाला ।

1758. He has fallen.
vo gir pa-Raa hai. वह गिर पड़ा है ।

1759. She has fainted.
vo bé-hosh ho ga-ee hai. वह बेहोश हो गई है ।

1760. Do not move her (OR: **him**).
[u-sé] hi-laa-i-yé na-heen. [उसे] हिलाइये नहीं ।

1761. [My finger] is bleeding.
[mé-ree ung-lee] sé khoon ni-kal ra-haa hai.
[मेरी उंगली] से खून निकल रहा है ।

1762. A fracture of [the arm].
[baan] kee Too-Tee haD-Dee. [बांह] की टूटी हड्डी ।

1763. I want [to rest] [to sit down] [to lie down].
mu-jhé [aa-raam kar-naa] [baiTH-naa] [léT-naa] hai.
मुझे [आराम करना] [बैठना] [लेटना] है ।

1764. Notify [my husband].
[mé-ré pa-tee] ko soo-chit kar dee-ji-yé.
[मेरे पति] को सूचित कर दीजिये ।

1765. A tourniquet.
rakt bandh. रक्त बन्ध ।

PARTS OF THE BODY

1766. Ankle.
Takh-naa. टखना ।

1767. Appendix.
uN-Duk (OR: a-pén-Diks). उण्डुक (अपेनडिक्स) ।

1768. Arm.
baan. बाँह ।

1769. Armpit.
kaankh. काँख ।

1770. Artery.
dham-nee. धमनी ।

1771. Back.
peeTH. पीठ ।

1772. Belly.
péT. पेट ।

1773. Blood.
rakt (OR: *khoon*). रक्त (खून) ।

1774. Blood vessel.
nas. नस ।

1775. Body.
sha-reer. शरीर ।

1776. Bone.
haD-Dee. हड्डी ।

1777. Bowel.
aant. आंत ।

1778. Brain.
di-maa*gh*. दिमाग ।

1779. Breast.
stan. स्तन ।

1780. Calf.
pinD-lee. पिंडली ।

1781. Cheek.
gaal. गाल ।

1782. Chest.
chhaa-tee. छाती ।

1783. Chin.
THuD-Dee. ठुड्डी ।

1784. Collarbone.
hans-lee. हंसली ।

1785. Ear.
kaan. कान ।

1786. Elbow.
ko-nee. कोहनी ।

1787. Eye.
$\overline{aa}$nkh. आँख ।

1788. Eyelashes.
ba-rau-ni-y$\overline{aa}$n. बरौनियाँ ।

1789. Eyelid.
pa-lak (OR: pa-po-Taa). पलक (पपोटा) ।

1790. Face.
m$\overline{u}$n (OR: chéh-raa). मुँह (चेहरा) ।

1791. Finger.
ung-lee. उंगली ।

1792. Fingernail.
naa-*khoon*. नाखून ।

1793. Foot.
pair (OR: paa-on). पैर (पाँव) ।

1794. Forehead.
maa-thaa. माथा ।

1795. Gall bladder.
pit-taa. पित्ता ।

1796. Genitals.
ja-nén dri-ya. जनेंद्रिय ।

1797. Glands.
gran-thee-ya (OR: gil-Tee).* ग्रन्थिय (गिल्टी) ।

1798. Gums.
ma-soo-Ré. मसूड़े ।

1799. Hair (on head).
baal. बाल ।

1800. Hair (on body).
rom. रोम ।

1801. Hand.
haath. हाथ ।

1802. Head.
sir. सिर ।

1803. Heart.
dil (OR: hri-day). दिल (हृदय) ।

1804. Heel.
é-Ree. एड़ी ।

---

* The second is more common for swollen glands.

1805. Hip.
kool-haa. कूल्हा ।

1806. Intestines.
aan-tén. आंतें ।

1807. Jaw.
jab-Raa. जबड़ा ।

1808. Joint.
joR. जोड़ ।

1809. Kidney.
gur-daa. गुरदा ।

1810. Knee.
ghuT-naa. घुटना ।

1811. Leg.
Taang. टाँग ।

1812. Lip.
honTH. होंठ ।

1813. Liver.
ka-lé-jaa. कलेजा ।

1814. Lung.
phéph-Raa. फेफड़ा ।

1815. Mouth.
mun. मुंह ।

1816. Muscle.
pé-shee. पेशी ।

1817. Navel.
naa-bhee. नाभी ।

1818. Neck.
gar-dan.   गरदन ।

1819. Nerve.
nas.   नस ।

1820. Nose.
naak.   नाक ।

1821. Palm.
ha-thé-lee.   हथेली ।

1822. Pancreas.
lab-la-baa.   लबलबा ।

1823. Rib.
pas-lee.   पसली ।

1824. Shoulder.
kan-dhaa.   कन्धा ।

1825. Side.
ba-*gha*l.   बग़ल ।

1826. Skin.
cham-Raa.   चमड़ा ।

1827. Skull.
khop-Ree.   खोपड़ी ।

1828. Sole.
tal-vaa.   तलवा ।

1829. Spine.
reeRH.   रीढ़ ।

1830. Spleen.
plee-haa.   प्लीहा ।

1831. Stomach.
péT. पेट।

1832. Temple.
kan-pa-Tee. कनपटी।

1833. Thigh.
jaangh. जांघ।

1834. Throat.
ga-laa. गला।

1835. Thumb.
an-goo-THaa. अंगूठा।

1836. Toe.
pair kee ung-lee. पैर की उंगली।

1837. Tongue.
jeebh. जीभ।

1838. Tonsils.
Taan-sil. टान्सिल।

1839. Vein.
rag (OR: nas). रग (नस)।

1840. Waist.
ka-mar. कमर।

1841. Wrist.
ka-laa-ee. कलाई।

TIME

1842. What time is it?
kit-né ba-jé hain (OR: kyaa sa-may hu-aa hai)?
कितने बजे हैं॰ (क्या समय हुआ है)?

1843. Two A.M.
raat ké do ba-jé. रात के दो बजे ।

1844. Two P.M.
din ké do ba-jé. दिन के दो बजे ।

1845. It is exactly half-past three.
THeek saa-RHé teen ba-jé hain.
ठीक साढ़े तीन बजे है ॑ ।

1846. Quarter-past four.
sa-vaa chaar ba-jé. सवा चार बजे ।

1847. Quarter to five.
pau-né paanch ba-jé. पौने पाँच बजे ।

1848. Ten minutes to six.
chhé baj-né men das mi-naT. छ: बजने में दस मिनट ।

1849. At twenty minutes past seven.
saat baj kar bees mi-naT par.
सात बज कर बीस मिनट पर ।

1850. It is early.
a-bhee jal-dee hai. अभी जल्दी है ।

1851. It is late.
dér ho chu-kee hai. देर हो चुकी है ।

1852. In the morning.
su-bah ko. सुबह को ।

1853. This afternoon.
aaj do-pa-har ko. आज दोपहर को ।

1854. Tomorrow.
kal. कल ।

1855. In the evening.
shaam ko. शाम को ।

1856. At noon.
din ké baa-raa ba-jé. दिन के बारह बजे।

1857. Midnight.
aa-dhee raat . आधी रात।

1858. During the day.
din mén. दिन में।

1859. Every night.
har raat. हर रात।

1860. All night.
saa-ree raat (OR: raat bhar). सारी रात (रात भर)।

1861. Since yesterday.
kal sé. कल से।

1862. Today.
aaj. आज।

1863. Tonight.
aaj raat. आज रात।

1864. Last month.
pichh-lé ma-hee-né. पिछले महीने।

1865. Last year.
pichh-lé saal. पिछले साल।

1866. Next Sunday.
ag-lé ra-vi-vaar ko. आगले रविवार को।

1867. Next week.
ag-lé haf-té (OR: sap-taah). आगले हफ्ते (सप्ताह)।

1868. The day before yesterday (OR: day after tomorrow).
par-son. परसों।

1869. Two weeks ago.
do haf-té péh-lé.   दो हफ़्ते पहले।

WEATHER

1870. How is the weather today?
aaj kaa mau-sam kai-saa hai?   आज का मौसम कैसा है?

1871. It looks like rain.
lag-taa hai ki baa-rish ho-gee.
लगता है कि बारिश होगी।

1872. It is [cold] [warm] [fair].
aaj [THanD] [ga-ram] [a-nu-kool] hai.
आज [ठंड] [गरम] [अनुकूल] है।

1873. It is windy.
ha-vaa chal ra-hee hai.   हवा चल रही है।

1874. The weather is clearing.
mau-sam saaf ho ra-haa hai.   मौसम साफ़ हो रहा है।

1875. What a beautiful day!
kit-naa su-haa-naa din hai.   कितना सुहाना दिन है।

1876. I want to sit in [the shade] [the sun] [a breeze].
main [chhaa-on] [dhoop] [ha-vaa] men baiTH-naa [chaa-ha-taa (M.)] [chaa-ha-tee (F.)] hoon.
मैं [छाँव] [धूप] [हवा] में बैठना [चाहता] [चाहती] हूँ।

1877. What is the weather forecast [for tomorrow]?
[kal kaa] mau-sam poor-vaa-nu-maan kyaa hai?
[कल का] मौसम पूर्वानुमान क्या है?

1878. —for the weekend.
—sap-taa-haant kaa.   _ सप्ताहान्त का।

1879. It will snow tomorrow.
kal barf pa-Ré-gee. कल बर्फ़ पड़ेगी ।

DAYS OF THE WEEK

1880. Sunday.
ra-vi-vaar. रविवार ।

1881. Monday.
som-vaar. सोमवार ।

1882. Tuesday.
man-gal-vaar. मंगलवार ।

1883. Wednesday.
budh-vaar. बुधवार ।

1884. Thursday.
bri-has-pa-ti-vaar. बृहस्पतिवार !

1885. Friday.
shu-kra-vaar. शुक्रवार ।

1886. Saturday.
sha-ni-vaar. शनिवार ।

HOLIDAYS

1887. A public holiday.
saarv-ja-nik chuT-Tee. सार्वजनिक छुट्टी ।

1888. [Merry] Christmas.
ba-Ré din [kee ba-dhaa-ee]. बड़े दिन [की बधाई] ।

1889. Happy Easter.
ees-Tar kee ba-dhaa-ee. ईस्टर की बधाई ।

1890. Happy New Year.
na-yé saal kee ba-dhaa-ee. नये साल की बधाई।

1891. Happy birthday.
ja-nam-din mu-baa-rak ho. जन्मदिन मुबारक हो।

1892. Happy anniversary.
varsh-gaanTH kee ba-dhaa-ee. वर्षगांठ की बधाई।

1893. A religious holiday.
tyo-haar. त्योहार।

1894. Happy Divali.*
di-vaa-lee kee ba-dhaa-ee. दिवाली की बधाई।

1895. Dussehra.†
da-séh-raa. दसहरा।

1896. Holi.‡
ho-lee. होली।

1897. Happy [Id].§
[eed] mu-baa-rak. [ईद] मुबारक।

DATES, MONTHS AND SEASONS

1898. January.
jan-va-ree. जनवरी।

1899. February.
far-va-ree. फ़रवरी।

* Hindu festival of lights.
† Hindu festival which includes a 10-day period of celebrations preceding Divali.
‡ Hindu festival where people throw colored powder and water at each other.
§ Moslem feast day.

1900. March.
maarch.　मार्च ।

1901. April.
a-prail.　अप्रैल ।

1902. May.
ma-ee.　मई ।

1903. June.
joon.　जून ।

1904. July.
ju-laa-ee.　जुलाई ।

1905. August.
a-gast.　अगस्त ।

1906. September.
si-tam-bar.　सितम्बर ।

1907. October.
ak-too-bar.　अकतूबर ।

1908. November.
na-vam-bar.　नवम्बर ।

1909. December.
di-sam-bar.　दिसम्बर ।

1910. The spring.
ba-sant.　बसन्त ।

1911. The summer.
gar-mee.　गरमी ।

1912. The autumn.
pat-jhaR.　पतझड़ ।

1913. The winter.
jaa-Raa.   जाड़ा ।

1914. The rainy season.
bar-saat.   बरसात ।

1915. Today is the 31st of May, [1980].
aaj ik-tees ma-ee [san un-nees sau as-see] hai.

आज इकतीस मई [सन उन्नीस सौ अस्सी] है ।

NUMBERS: CARDINALS

1916. Zero.*
shoon-ya.   शून्य (०) ।

1917. One.
ék.   एक (१) ।

1918. Two.
do.   दो (२) ।

1919. Three.
teen.   तीन (३) ।

1920. Four.
chaar.   चार (४) ।

1921. Five.
paanch.   पांच (५) ।

1922. Six.
chhé.   छः (६) ।

1923. Seven.
saat.   सात (७) ।

* The Hindi numerals 0-10 are included for reference and recognition.

1924. Eight.
aaTH.   आठ (८)।

1925. Nine.
nau.   नौ (९)।

1926. Ten.
das.   दस (१०)।

1927. Eleven.
gyaa-raa.   ग्यारह।

1928. Twelve.
baa-raa.   बारह।

1929. Thirteen.
té-raa.   तेरह।

1930. Fourteen.
chau-daa.   चौदह।

1931. Fifteen.
pan-draa.   पन्द्रह।

1932. Sixteen.
so-laa.   सोलह।

1933. Seventeen.
sat-ta-raa.   सत्तरह।

1934. Eighteen.
a-THaa-raa.   अठारह।

1935. Nineteen.
un-nees.   उन्नीस।

1936. Twenty.
bees.   बीस।

1937. Twenty-one.
ik-kees.   इक्कीस ।

1938. Twenty-five.
pach-chees.   पच्चीस ।

1939. Twenty-nine.
un-tees.   उनतीस ।

1940. Thirty.
tees.   तीस ।

1941. Thirty-five.
pain-tees.   पैंतीस ।

1942. Thirty-nine.
un-chaa-lees.   उनचालीस ।

1943. Forty.
chaa-lees.   चालीस ।

1944. Forty-five.
pain-taa-lees.   पैंतालीस ।

1945. Forty-nine.
un-chaas.   उनचास ।

1946. Fifty.
pa-chaas.   पचास ।

1947. Fifty-five.
pach-pan.   पच्पन ।

1948. Fifty-nine.
un-saTH.   उनसठ ।

1949. Sixty.
saaTH.   साठ ।

1950. Sixty-five.
pain-saTH.   पैंसठ ।

1951. Sixty-nine.
un-hat-tar.   उनहत्तर ।

1952. Seventy.
sat-tar.   सत्तर ।

1953. Seventy-five.
pach-hat-tar.   पचहत्तर ।

1954. Seventy-nine.
un-naa-see.   उन्नासी ।

1955. Eighty.
as-see.   अस्सी ।

1956. Eighty-five.
pa-chaa-see.   पचासी ।

1957. Eighty-nine.
na-vaa-see.   नवासी ।

1958. Ninety.
nab-bé.   नब्बे ।

1959. Ninety-five.
pa-chaan-vé.   पचानवे ।

1960. Ninety-nine.
nin-yaan-vé.   निन्यानवे ।

1961. One hundred.
ék sau.   एक सौ ।

1962. One hundred and one.
ék sau ék.   एक सौ एक ।

1963. One thousand.
ék ha-zaar. एक हज़ार ।

1964. One hundred thousand.
ék laakh. एक लाख ।

1965. One million.
das laakh. दस लाख ।

1966. Ten million.
ék ka-roR. एक करोड़ ।

NUMBERS: ORDINALS

1967. The first.*
[péh-laa (M.)] [péh-lee (F.)] [péh-lé (PL.)].
[पहला] [पहली] [पहले] ।

1968. The second.
doos-raa. दूसरा ।

1969. The third.
tees-raa. तीसरा ।

1970. The fourth.
chau-thaa. चौथा ।

1971. The fifth.*
[p̄aanch-vaan (M.)] [p̄aanch-veen (F.)] [p̄aanch-vén (PL.)].
[पांचवाँ] [पांचवी] [पांचवें] ।

---

* The ordinal numbers behave as adjectives and the endings change according to whether the noun is masculine, feminine, singular or plural. The first entry is an example of one set of endings (non-nasalized), and the fifth entry of the other set (nasalized).

1972. The sixth.
chha-THaa.   छठा ।

1973. The seventh.*
saat-vaan.   सातवाँ ।

1974. The eighth.
aaTH-vaan.   आठवाँ ।

1975. The ninth.
nau-vaan.   नौवाँ ।

1976. The tenth.
das-vaan.   दसवाँ ।

1977. The twentieth.
bees-vaan.   बीसवाँ ।

1978. The thirtieth.
tees-vaan.   तीसवाँ ।

1979. The hundredth.
sau-vaan.   सौवाँ ।

1980. The thousandth.
ha-zaar-vaan.   हज़ारवाँ ।

QUANTITIES

1981. A fraction.
bhinn.   भिन्न ।

1982. A quarter.
chau-thaa-ee (OR: paa-o).   चौथाई (पाव) ।

---

* All ordinals after this take the second set of endings.

1983. A third.
ti-haa-ee. तिहाई ।

1984. A half.
aa-dhaa. आधा ।

1985. Three-quarters.
teen chau-thaa-ee. तीन चौथाई ।

1986. One and one quarter.
sa-vaa. सवा ।

1987. One and one half.
DéRH. डेढ़ ।

1988. Two and one half.
a-RHaa-ee. अढ़ाई ।

1989. Three and one half.
saa-RHé teen. साढ़े तीन ।

1990. Three and three-quarters.
pau-né chaar. पौने चार ।

1991. The whole.
poo-raa. पूरा ।

1992. A pair.
ék jo-Raa. एक जोड़ा ।

1993. A few.
kuchh. कुछ ।

1994. Several.
ka-ee (OR: a-nék). कई (अनेक) ।

1995. Many.
ba-hut. बहुत ।

FAMILY*

1996. Wife.
pat-nee (OR: stree). पत्नी (स्त्री) ।

1997. Husband.
pa-tee. पति ।

1998. Mother.
maa-taa (OR: m$\overline{aa}$n). मातता (माँ) ।

1999. Father.
pi-taa (OR: baap). पिता (बाप) ।

2000. Parents.
m$\overline{aa}$n-baap. माँ-बाप ।

2001. Maternal grandmother.
naa-nee. नानी ।

2002. Maternal grandfather.
naa-naa. नाना ।

2003. Paternal grandmother.
daa-dee. दादी ।

2004. Paternal grandfather.
daa-daa. दादा ।

2005. Daughter.
bé-Tee. बेटी ।

* The family unit in India is extremely important. Families are generally large and close and relationships are more accurately defined by terms than in English. Often the suffix -*jee* is added to the end of a term as a sign of respect and affection, e.g. *maata* becomes *maataajee*, *pitaa* becomes *pitaajee*, etc.

2006. Son.
bé-Taa. बेटा ।

2007. Sister.
ba-hén. बहन ।

2008. Brother.
bhaa-ee. भाई ।

2009. Aunt (father's sister).
boo-aa (OR: phoo-phee). बूआ (फूफी) ।

2010. Aunt (mother's sister).
mau-see. मौसी ।

2011. Aunt (father's brother's wife).
chaa-chee. चाची ।

2012. Aunt (mother's brother's wife).
maa-mee. मामी ।

2013. Uncle (father's brother).
chaa-chaa. चाचा ।

2014. Uncle (mother's brother).
maa-maa. मामा ।

2015. Uncle (father's sister's husband).
phoo-phaa. फूफा ।

2016. Uncle (mother's sister's husband).
mau-saa. मौसा ।

2017. Niece (brother's daughter).
bha-tee-jee. भतीजी ।

2018. Niece (sister's daughter).
bhaan-jee. भांजी ।

2019. Nephew (brother's son).
bha-tee-jaa.   भतीजा ।

2020. Nephew (sister's son).
bhaan-jaa.   भांजा ।

2021. Cousin.
[bhaa-ee (M.)] [ba-hén (F.)].   [भाई] [बहन] ।

2022. Mother-in-law.
saas.   सास ।

2023. Father-in-law.
sa-sur.   ससुर ।

2024. Relatives.
rish-té-daar.   रिश्तेदार ।

2025. Adults.
bu-zurg.   बुजुर्ग ।

2026. Children.
baal-bach-ché.   बाल-बच्चे ।

COMMON SIGNS & PUBLIC NOTICES

2027. Admission.
pra-vésh.   प्रवेश ।

2028. (Admission) free.
muft.   मुफ्त ।

2029. Air conditioned.
vaa-taa-noo-koo-lit.   वातानुकूलित ।

2030. Attention.
saav-dhaan.   सावधान।

2031. Bathing prohibited.
na-haa-naa ma-naa hai.   नहाना मना है।

2032. Beware of dog.
saav-dhaan kut-taa *kha*-tar-naak hai.
सावधान कुत्ता ख़तरनाक है।

2033. Bus stop.
bas aD-Daa.   बस अड्डा।

2034. Business school.
kaa-mars kaa-lij.   कामर्स कालिज।

2035. Cemetery.
ka-bri-staan.   कब्रिस्तान।

2036. City hall.
na-gar paa-li-kaa kaa daf-tar.   नगर पालिका का दफ़्तर।

2037. Clinic.
kli-nik.   क्लिनिक।

2038. Closed for vacation.
chhuT-Tee ké li-yé band hai.
छुट्टी के लिये बन्द है।

2039. Closed from 8 P.M. to 9 A.M.
aaTH ba-jé raat sé nau ba-jé su-bah tak band ra-hé-gaa.
आठ बजे रात से नौ बजे सुबह तक बन्द रहेगा।

2040. Closed on Sundays [and holidays].
ra-vi-vaar [aur chhuT-Tee ké din] band ra-hé-gaa.
रविवार [और छुट्टी के दिन] बन्द रहेगा।

2041. Cold.
THanD. ठंड।

2042. Continuous performance.
a-khanD aa-yo-jan. अखंड आयोजन।

2043. Danger.
*kh*at-raa. ख़तरा।

2044. Departure.
ra-vaan-gee (OR: pra-sthaan). रवानगी (प्रस्थान)।

2045. Diner.
bho-ja-naa-lay. भोजनालय।

2046. Do not feed the animals.
jaan-va-r̄on ko khaa-naa dé-naa ma-naa hai.
जानवरों को ख़ाना देना मना है।

2047. Down.
nee-ché. नीचे।

2048. Elevator.
lifT. लिफ़्ट।

2049. Emergency exit.
aa-paa-tee dvaar. आपाती द्वार।

2050. Employees only.
ké-val karm-chaa-ri-ȳon ké li-yé.
केवल कर्मचारियों के लिये।

2051. Engaged (OR: **Occupied**).
vyast. व्यस्त।

2052. Enter.
an-dar. अन्दर।

2053. Entrance.
pra-vésh. प्रवेश ।

2054. Exit.
ni-kaas. निकास ।

2055. Factory.
kaar-*khaa*-naa. कारख़ाना ।

2056. Fixed price.
nis-chit daam. निश्चित दाम ।

2057. Forbidden.
ma-naa (OR: ni-shédh). मना (निषेध) ।

2058. For sale.
bi-kaa-oo. बिकाऊ ।

2059. For hire (OR: **rent**).
ki-raa-yé ké li-yé. किराये के लिये ।

2060. Free.
muft. मुफ़्त ।

2061. Furnished rooms for rent.
sa-jé kam-ré ki-raa-yé ké li-yé. सजे कमरे किराये के लिये ।

2062. Gentlemen (OR: **Men**).
pu-rush. पुरुष ।

2063. Government house.
raaj-bha-van. राजभवन ।

2064. Hospital.
as-pa-taal. अस्पताल ।

2065. Hot.
ga-ram. गरम ।

2066. House for rent.

ma-kaan ki-raa-yé ké li-yé hai. मकान किरायॆ के लिॆ है।

2067. Information.

poochh-taachh. पूछ-ताछ।

2068. Janitor.

ja-maa-daar. जमादार।

2069. Keep off the grass.

ghaas par chal-naa ma-naa hai.

घास पर चलना मना है।

2070. Ladies' waiting room.

ma-hi-laa pra-tee-kshaa-lay. महिला प्रतीक्षालय।

2071. Ladies' room.

ma-hi-laa shau-chaa-lay. महिला शौचालय।

2072. Library.

pus-ta-kaa-lay. पुस्तकालय।

2073. Men's room.

aad-mi-yōn kaa shau-chaa-lay. आदमियॊं का शौचालय।

2074. Men at work.

kaam chaa-loo hai. काम चालू है।

2075. No admittance [except on business].

[bi-naa za-roo-rat] an-dar aa-né kee i-jaa-zat na-heen hai.

[बिना ज़रूरत] अन्दर आने की इजाज़त नहीं है।

2076. No noise.

shor mat kee-ji-yé. शोर मत कीजिॆ।

2077. No performance.

khél na-heen ho-gaa. खेल नहीं होगा।

2078. No smoking.
dhu-mar-paan ni-shédh hai.   धुम्रपान निषेध है।

2079. No spitting.
thook-naa ma-naa hai.   थूकना मना है।

2080. No swimming.
tair-naa ma-naa hai.   तैरना मना है।

2081. No trespassing (OR: **No thoroughfare**).
aam raas-taa na-heen hai.   आम रास्ता नहीं है।

2082. Notices.
sooch-naa-yén.   सूचनायें।

2083. Occupied.
*kh*aa-lee na-heen.   खाली नहीं।

2084. On sale here.
ya-haan bik-taa hai.   यहाँ बिकता है।

2085. Open.
khu-laa.   खुला।

2086. Open from 9 A.M. to 8 P.M.
nau ba-jé sé lé-kar aaTH ba-jé tak khu-laa ra-hé-gaa.
नौ बजे से लेकर आठ बजे तक खुला रहेगा।

2087. Pedestrians [only].
[ké-val] pai-dal raas-taa.   [केवल] पैदल रास्ता।

2088. Police.
pu-lis.   पुलिस।

2089. Post no bills.
vi-gyaa-pan la-gaa-naa ni-shédh hai.
विज्ञापन लगाना निषेध है।

2090. Private road.
aam raas-taa na-heen hai. आम रास्ता नहीं है।

2091. Public notice.
saarv-ja-nik sooch-naa. सार्वजनिक सूचना।

2092. Public telephone.
saarv-ja-nik Té-lee-fon. सार्वजनिक टेलीफ़ोन।

2093. Pull.
kheen-chi-yé. खींचिये।

2094. Push.
dhak-kaa dee-ji-yé. धक्का दीजिये।

2095. Quiet.
chup (OR: *khaa*-mosh). चुप (ख़ामोश)।

2096. Railroad station.
rél-vé i-sTé-shan. रेलवे इस्टेशन।

2097. Refreshments.
jal-paan. जलपान।

2098. Refuse.
koo-Raa. कूड़ा।

2099. Reserved.
aa-ra-kshit. आरक्षित।

2100. Retail.
khud-raa. खुदरा।

2101. Ring the bell.
ghan-Tee ba-jaa-i-yé. घंटी बजाइये।

2102. Discount sale.
chhooT par maal. छूट पर माल।

2103. Self-service.
sva-yam-sé-vaa. स्वयंसेवा ।

2104. Silence (OR: **No talking**).
baat kar-naa ma-naa hai. बात करना मना है ।

2105. Smoking forbidden.
tam-baa-koo pee-naa ma-naa hai.
तम्बाकू पीना मना है ।

2106. Stairs.
see-RHi-yaan. सीढ़ियाँ ।

2107. Taxi stand.
Taik-see aD-Daa. टैक्सी अड्डा ।

2108. Telephone.
Té-lee-fon. टेलीफ़ोन ।

2109. Television.
Té-lee-vi-zan. टेलीविज़न ।

2110. Ticket office.
Ti-kaT-ghar. टिकटघर ।

2111. Toilet.
shau-chaa-lay. शौचालय ।

2112. Up.
oo-par. ऊपर ।

2113. Vacant.
*kh*aa-lee. ख़ाली ।

2114. Waiting room.
pra-tee-kshaa-lay. प्रतीक्षालय ।

2115. Warning.
ché-taa-va-nee. चेतावनी ।

2116. Watch your step.

dhyaan sé cha-li-yé.   ध्यान से चलिये।

2117. Wet paint.

rang gee-laa hai.   रंग गिला है।

2118. Wholesale.

thok ké hi-saab.   थोक के हिसाब।

2119. Will return at [1 P.M.].

[do-pa-har ké ék ba-jé] lau-ten̄-gé.

[दोपहर के एक बजे] लौटेंगे।

2120. Zoo.

chi-Ri-yaa-ghar.   चिड़ियाघर।

INDEX

The phrases in this book are numbered consecutively from 1 to 2120. Entries in this index refer to these numbers. Each section heading (capitalized) and subsection heading (in small capitals) is indexed according to page number. Parts of speech are indicated (where there might be confusion) by italic abbreviations: *adj.* for adjective, *adv.* for adverb, *n.* for noun, *prep.* for preposition, and *v.* for verb. Parentheses are used for explanations.

Because of the large extent of the material, cross-indexing has been avoided. Phrases of two or more words will be found under only one of their components. If you do not find a phrase under one of its words, try another.

Every English word is followed by its Hindi equivalent, given in dictionary form (the masculine singular in the nominative case for nouns and adjectives, and the infinitive for verbs). Thus, the reader is provided with a basic English–Hindi glossary. Naturally, an acquaintance with Hindi grammar is helpful for making the best use of this index, but not necessary, as it is designed to be a productive tool for speakers at all levels. To assist you in using the correct forms of words in your own sentences, the index lists not only the first sentence in which each word occurs, but also those in which the basic form is significantly altered.

Invariable words or those with no significant variations are indexed only under their first appearance, and only one occurrence of each variation is given. The beginner should look at all the sentences listed for a word to become familiar with the different shades of meaning of all the Hindi equivalents listed for a single English entry.

Syllabification and the Hindi script should also be referred to in the original numbered entry.

Where a numbered sentence contains a choice of Hindi equivalents, only the first choice has been included.

(Symbols which are italicized in the text, i.e., *kh, gh,* are indicated in the index by *kh, gh.*)

beside (*prep.*): *ké baghal* 210

best: *sab sé achchhaa* 528

betel (leaf): *paan* 1494; — nut: *supaaree* 1493

better: *béhtar* 567; *zyaadaa achchhaa* 1666

between (*prep.*): *ké beech* 200

BEVERAGES AND BREAKFAST FOODS, p. 77

beware: *saavdhaan* 2032

beyond (*prep.*): *ké aagé* 201

bib: *gatiyaa* 1638

bicarbonate of soda: *soDaa baaee kaarb* 1378

bicycle: *saaikil* 347

big: *baRaa* 1189

bill (banknote): *noT* 1145; (check): *bil* 565; (advertising poster): *vigyaapan* 2089

birthday: *janamdin* 1891

bit (a little): *zaraa* 23

bite: *kaaTnaa* 1696

bitter melon: *karélaa* 865

black: *kaalaa* 169

blanket: *kambal* 613

bleed: *khoon nikalnaa* 1761

blister: *chhaalaa* 1697

block: *blaak* 203

blood: *rakt* 1773; — vessel: *nas* 1774

blouse: *cholee* 1231

blue: *neelaa* 1294

board (*v.*): *chaRHnaa* 265; go on — (boat): *jahaaz par chaRHnaa* 225

boarding pass: *vimaan patra* 272

BOAT, p. 23

bobby pin: *chimTee* 1379

body: *shareer* 1775

boil (*n.*): *phoRaa* 1698

boiled: *ublaa huaa* 735

bolt: *péch* 403

bone: *haDDee* 1776

book (*n.*): *pustak* 1043; *kitaab* 1331; (*v.*, reserve): *jagah lénaa* 992

bookshop: *kitaab kee dukaan* 1569

BOOKSHOP, STATIONER & NEWSDEALER, p. 125

boot: *jootaa* 1232

bored, be: *jee oob jaanaa* 1026

boric acid: *borik paauDar* 1380

botanical garden: *baageechaa* 1019

bother (*v.*, take trouble): *kashT karnaa* 14; (annoy): *tang karnaa* 136

bottle: *botal* 683, 1640; —

cabbage: *band gobhee* 866

cabin: *kaibin* 236; —
steward: *kaibin bairaa*
242

cablegram: *vidéshee taar*
497

CAFÉ AND BAR, p. 66

cake: *kék* 935

Calcutta: *kalkattaa* 245

calf (of leg): *pinDlee* 1780

call (n.): *fon* 526; (v.):
bulaanaa 267, 1626; (on
telephone): *fon karnaa*
504, 524, 525

camera: *kaimraa* 1446

CAMERA SHOP AND
PHOTOGRAPHY, p.
135

camping: *shivir* 1121

campsite: *shivir sthaan*
1120

can (n.): *Teen* 723; (v.):
saknaa 101, 163, 1068;
paanaa 1206

cancel: *radd karvaanaa*
244

candle: *mombattee* 617

candy: *barfee* 982;
miTHaaee 1463; —
shop: *miTHaaee kee
dukaan* 1571

cane: *chhaRee* 1238

can opener: *Teen kholné
vaalaa* 641

cap: *Topee* 1239

captain: *kaptaan* 240

car: *moTar gaaRee* 333;
gaaRee 342; *moTar* 372;
(of train): *Dibbaa* 299

caramel custard: *kairaamal
kasTarD* 936

carbon paper: *kaarban*
1347

carburetor: *kaarbooréTar*
407

cardamom: *ilaaychee* 768

cards (playing): *taash*
1096

careful: *saavdhaan* 29

carefully: *sambhaal kar*
178; *dhyaan sé* 324;
saavdhaanee sé 1219

carom: *kairam* 1102

carpet: *kaaleen* 663

carriage: *praim* 1634

carrot: *gaajar* 867

carry (take): *lénaa* 171

cashew: *kaajoo* 908

cashier: *khazaanchee* 759

castle: *kilaa* 1016

catsup: *TamaaTar saas* 790

cauliflower: *phool gobhee*
868

caution: *saavdhaan* 1365

cave: *guhaa* 1012

cavity, have a: *keeRaa
lagnaa* 1749

celery: *sélaree* 869

cemetery: *kabristan* 2035

center: *beech* 186

Centigrade: *sénTeegréD* 1440

ceramics: *cheenee miTTee* 1322

cereal (hot): *daliyaa* 810; (cold): *kaurn fléks* 811

certificate: *pramaaNpatra* 149

chair: *kursee* 226

change (n.): *baaqee paisé* 763; *khulé paisé* 1147; (v.): *badalnaa* 311, 377, 614

charge (n.): *daam* 507; *kiraayaa* 994; (v., take money): *lénaa* 317

chassis: *chésis* 408

cheap: *sastaa* 568

check (n.): *chék* 1142; (bill): *bil* 758; (v.): *chék karnaa* 382; — through (send): *bhéjnaa* 163; — out (of room): *khalee karnaa* 602

checkroom: *asbaab-ghar* 1572

cheek: *gaal* 1781

cheese: *paneer* 947

cheroot: *beeRee* 1492

chess: *shatranj* 1101

chest (body): *chhaatee* 1782; — of drawers: *kapRon kaa daraaz* 643

chewing gum: *chooing gam* 1381

chewing tobacco: *tambaakoo kee pattee* 1490

chicken: *murgee* 822; — in butter and tomato sauce: *makkhanee murg* 958; whole roast —: *murg musallam* 959; — and onion curry: *murgee do pyaazaa* 960; marinated, grilled —: *tandooree murgaa* 961

chicken pox: *chéchak* 1701

chickpea(s): *chanaa* 891; — flour: *bésan* 902; curried —: *kaablee chanaa* 967

child: *bachchaa* 2026

chill: *jooRee* 1702

chin: *THuDDee* 1783

china: *cheeneę ké bartan* 1323

choke (n.): *chok* 409

cholera: *haizaa* 1703

chop: *chaup* 830

chopped: *kaTaa huaa* 736; — meat: *qeemaa* 945; — meat and lentil patty: *shaamee kabaab* 957

choral music: *samvét bhajan* 1036

Christian: *eesaaee* 1056

Christmas: *baRaa din* 1888

matter (n.): baat 52

matter, it doesn't: koee
baat naheen 13

May: maee 1902

me: mujhé 168

meal: bhojan 559; khaanaa
706

meaning: arth 119

measles: khasraa 1725

measurements: naap 1191

meat: maans 821; gosht
950

MEAT ENTREES, p. 91

MEATS, p. 80

meatball: koftaa 837

mechanic: moTar mistree
373

mechanism: yantra 343

medication: davaa 1361

medicine dropper:
Draapar 1411

medium: madhyam 384

meet: milnaa 30, 33

melon: kharboozaa 919

men's room: aadmiyon kaa
shauchaalay 2073

menthol: ménthol 1479

menu: bhojan soochee
708

message: sandésh 523

messenger: sandéshvaahak
595

metal: dhaatu 1306

meter: meeTar 1156

middle: beechobeech 203;
beech 1539

midnight: aadhee raat
1857

mild: halkaa 1361

milk: doodh 797

millet: baajraa 896

milliner: Topee banaané
vaalaa 1599

million (one): das laakh
1965; ten —: ék karoR
1966

mine: méraa 152

mineral water: chashmé
kaa paanee 677

minimum: kam sé kam 499

mint: pudeenaa 777

minute: minaT 329

mirror: sheeshaa 448

Miss: kumaaree 31

missing, be: kam honaa
166

mistake: ghaltee 761

modern: adhunik 1009

Monday: somvaar 1545

money: paisé 1140; —
exchange: paisé badalné
kee dukaan 1600; —
order: manee aarDar
491

month: maheenaa 564

monument: smaarak 211

more: zyaadaa 572; aur
747

morning: *subah* 585
Moslem: *musalmaan* 1058
mosque: *masjid* 185
mosquito net: *masahree* 658
mother: *maataa* 1998
mother-in-law: *saas* 2022
motor: *injan* 393; — scooter: *iskooTar* 349
motorcycle: *faTfaTiyaa* 348
mountain: *pahaaR* 995
mouth: *mūn* 1815; — wash: *kullaa karné kee davaa* 1413
move (*v.*): *hilaanaa* 1760
movies: *sinémaa* 1083
Mr.: *shree* 32; *saahab* 77
Mrs.: *shreematee* 30
mud: *keechaR* 378
muffler: *saailénsar* 450
mumps: *kanpéRaa* 1726
muscle: *péshee* 1816
museum: *sangrahaalay* 1027
mushroom: *khumee* 874; black dried —: *guchchhee* 875
music: *sangeet* 1085; — store: *vaadhyayantrōn kee dukaan* 1601
musical instrument: *vaadhyayantra* 1602
must: *paRnaa* 153
mustache: *mōonchhēn* 1541

mustard: *raaee* 778; — greens: *sarsōn kaa saag* 885
mutton: *bakré kaa gosht* 838; — curry: *rogan josh* 954; — in yogurt gravy: *shaahee kormaa* 956
my: *méraa* 47, 134, 149; *apnaa* 165
myself: *svayam* 173

nail (metal): *keel* 451; — file: *naakhoon-rétee* 1414; — polish: *naakhoon kee paalish* 1415
name: *naam* 76
napkin: *naipkin* 711
native (*adj.*): *déshee* 1008
nausea: *matlee* 1727
navel: *naabhee* 1817
near (*adj.*): *paas* 190; (*prep.*): *ké paas* 206
nearest: *sab sé paas* 379
necessary: *aavashyak* 1662
neck: *gardan* 1818
necklace: *haar* 158
necktie: *Taaee* 1251
need (*v.*): *chaahiyé* 1109
needle: *sooee* 1527
needlework: *kasheedaa* 1469
negative (*n.*): *nigéTiv* 1458
nephew (brother's son):

ointment: *marham* 1417
okra: *bhinDee* 876; — and
  meat curry: *bhinDee
  gosht* 950
old: *pracheen* 1001
olive: *zaitoon* 877; — .
  green: *khaakee* 1298
omelet: *aamlét* 817
on: *par* 89; *ké baghal* 262
one: *ék* 91; — and one
  quarter: *savaa* 1986; —
  and one half: *DéRH*
  1987
one-way: *ék taraf* 292
onion: *pyaaz* 878
only: *kéval* 107
open (*adj.*): *khulaa* 2085;
  (*v.*): *kholnaa* 153, 284;
  khulnaa 154, 273, 346,
  1027
operate (work): *chalnaa*
  344
operation: *aapréshan* 1662
operator (telephone):
  aapréTar 503
opposite (*prep.*): *ké saamné*
  209
or: *yaa* 116; *ki* 190
orange (*n.*): *santaraa* 804;
  maalTaa 920; (color):
  naarangee kaa rang 1299
orchestra seat: *neeché kee
  seeT* 1066
order (*v.*): *mangvaanaa*
  754, 1181

orlon: *aurlaan* 1319
orthopedist: *haDDiyōn kaa
  DaakTar* 1687
other: *doosraa* 197
our: *hamaaraa* 146; *apnaa*
  132
out: *baahar* 1028
outdoors: *baahar* 698
outside (*adj.*): *baahar* 546;
  (*prep.*): *ké baahar* 207
overnight: *raat bhar* 361
over there: *udhar* 152
own (*v.*): *ké paas honaa*
  169
oxcart: *bail gaaRee* 351
oysters: *shukti* 855

pacifier: *choosnee* 1632
pack (*n.*): *Dibbee* 1480;
  (*v.*): *paik karnaa* 1219
package: *poTlee* 166;
  paarsal 485; *Dibbiyaa*
  1159
pail: *baalTee* 659
pain: *dard* 1652
paint: *rang* 2117
painting (art): *chitrakalaa*
  1006
paint store: *rang kee
  dukaan* 1604
pair: *joRaa* 1992
pajamas (Western-style):
  soné ké kapRé 1253;
  (Indian trousers):
  paijaamaa 1254